DIGITAL
MARKETING

2 / YOUR ADVISOR

DIGITAL MARKETING

RACHEL KILLEEN

CHARTERED
ACCOUNTANTS
IRELAND

Published in 2018 by
Chartered Accountants Ireland
Chartered Accountants House
47–49 Pearse Street
Dublin 2
www.charteredaccountants.ie

ISBN 978-1-910374-39-9

Typeset by PH Media
Printed by GRAFO, S.A.

For Celine O'Donovan and Brian Horgan

CONTENTS

ACKNOWLEDGEMENTS

Throughout the writing of this book, I felt very fortunate in discussing the topic with so many talented people who excel in digital marketing for their businesses. It is those excellent people that I have to thank for the content of this book. Thank you to Daragh Anglim, Fáilte Ireland; Teresa Phelan, The Little Milk Company; Padraig O'Neill, 123.ie; Fabio Molle, Funky Christmas Jumpers; Marie Collier, VHI; Brian Horgan, Abbey Theatre; Sally-Ann Collier, Howth Haven; Jessie Zhang and Lucy Woolford, Kong Digital; Steve McGettigan, Sims IVF, Gerard O'Neill, Amárach Consulting; David Curtin, IEDR; and Ursula Finlay. Thanks in particular to Robert Kelly, Kong Digital, who provided insights and analysis of work at the forefront of digital marketing.

Digital Marketing has received unwavering support from two exemplary people at Chartered Accountants Ireland: Michael Diviney, Director of Publishing, and Liz Riley, Editor. Thank you both for your support, feedback and input, which have helped shape this book into one of the innovative Your Advisor series.

In writing any book, there is an input of time and often that extends to family time. I am also fortunate to have the support of my husband Michael Torpey, the girls – Julie and Eimear – my mother Sheila and mother-in-law Kitty. Thanks to Chonalyn Abrique who helped so much on the administration side. Thanks also to Celine, Brian, Gráinne and Laura for support along the way.

INTRODUCTION
DIGITAL REVOLUTION

"The Digital revolution and the explosion of social media have profoundly changed what influences consumers as they undertake their purchasing decision journey."
Measuring Marketing's Worth, *McKinsey Quarterly*, May 2012

Your customers are online

Obermutten, a remote Swiss village with 79 inhabitants, launches a Facebook campaign that gets more interaction than Lady Gaga and more fans than the city of Florence (see **Chapter 4**). Hailo (now called mytaxi) cabs launch an app that reinvents the entire taxi service model and now there's one hailed online every two seconds around Europe (see **Chapter 7**). Funky Christmas Jumpers' online store gets a global order-boost when Niall Horan of One Direction tweets them a thank you (see **Chapter 10**). These stories reveal that digital marketing can work, but how do you make digital marketing work for your business?

On 11 August 1994, Sting's album, *Ten Summoner's Tales,* was the first item to be sold online and it was sold by Dan Kohn via a website called NetMarket – the first encrypted transaction across the web. Today, 94% of Irish Internet users shop online, according to the Virgin Media Digital Insights Report 2018. Currently, Irish SMEs are missing out, with about 60% of consumer online spending going to retailers marketing from abroad. Online marketing works, but how does it work? In this book, I will attempt to answer the following 'how' questions:

How does digital marketing work?

How can you make digital marketing work for your business?

Digital marketing works because it works for customers. People can buy online from the back seat of a New York cab, from the top of a Dublin double-decker bus or from a fast-ferry in Sydney Harbour. You can buy virtually anything, virtually anywhere – virtually.

Customers now have the tools, ranging from Internet search engines such as Google, to social media networks like Facebook, Instagram and Twitter and the devices, including smart-phones, tablets and PCs that they need to exercise a power they never had before. It's called consumer power and it is very powerful indeed.

First it was fuelled by the Internet, then by social media and now it is crowd-sourced for, user-generated content power. Consumer power can be your enemy or your friend – if you're in business, you have to mobilise that power in order to drive your success.

Your aim is to drive people to your online eco-system. Capture them with high-quality social media interactions, hold them with a highly relevant, content-laden website and build their loyalty with superb online micro-moments that are abundant in information, relevance and personalised content.

What is digital marketing?

Digital marketing makes use of electronic devices such as computers, tablets, smartphones, smart televisions and digital billboards. Digital marketing utilises online chat, email, advertising, websites, mobile apps, gaming, artificial intelligence such as chatbots, video, live-streaming and social media. A digital marketing asset suite also includes search engine optimisation (SEO), search marketing and web analytics. Going beyond the Internet, digital marketing extends to digital outdoor display advertising and TV screens in public places such as hospitals, stadiums and leisure facilities. Only very large companies use all of these tools – you should choose the ones that make sense for your business.

Digital marketing is definitely trending

Traditional marketing uses printed advertising and literature, as well as broadcast media such as radio, and television. Marketers globally have moved much of their marketing spend from traditional customer engagement to influence and track their behaviour online, and then to **measure** return on investment. Traditional marketing channels are typically more difficult to measure – despite best efforts. With digital, results are more immediate and arguably better value for money.

On the other hand, traditional marketing approaches help to build brand awareness and it is difficult to attract customers online unless you have a recognisable brand. Throughout this book, I recommend an integrated marketing approach, which uses a mix of both traditional and digital marketing methods to promote your brand. So don't close your physical store just yet. Don't dump the brochures or halt the radio advertising. While building your brand, you may also find that printing and/or broadcasting your message works to drive consumers to your online channels.

DIGITAL MARKETING – THE FACTS

ONE IN FIVE IRISH SMES HAVE NO ONLINE PRESENCE*

88% OF IRISH CUSTOMERS RESEARCH ONLINE BEFORE BUYING*

CONSUMERS ARE MORE LIKELY TO PURCHASE FROM A BUSINESS THAT HAS AN ONLINE PRESENCE**

ONLY 40% OF SME WEBSITES CAN TAKE SALES ORDERS**

ONLY 34% OF SMES CAN PROCESS PAYMENTS ONLINE**

74% OF SMES DO NOT ENGAGE IN E-COMMERCE. MANY SAY THEY DON'T HAVE SALES VOLUMES TO MAKE IT VIABLE AND ARE CONCERNED ABOUT RED TAPE, SHIPPING AND FRAUD**

THE INCREASE IN IRISH CONSUMER SPENDING IN 2017 WAS DRIVEN PURELY BY E-COMMERCE (+7.4% YEAR ON YEAR), AS FACE-TO-FACE SPENDING IS FLAT (0%).***

IRELAND'S SHARE OF THE EUROPEAN E-COMMERCE MARKETPLACE IS WORTH €9 BN. BY 2021, THAT IS EXPECTED TO RISE TO €14 BN****

SOURCES: *INDECON INTERNATIONAL ECONOMIC CONSULTANTS REPORT 'ASSESSMENT OF THE MACRO-ECONOMIC IMPACT OF INTERNET/DIGITAL ON THE IRISH ECONOMY' (MARCH 2016)

**IEDR DOT IE DIGITAL HEALTH INDEX RESEARCHED BY IGNITE RESEARCH (Q4 2017)

***VISA EUROPE IRISH CONSUMER SPENDING INDEX (FEBRUARY 2018)

****VIRGIN MEDIA DIGITAL INSIGHTS REPORT (JANUARY 2018)

The digital marketing revolution

Research tells us that customers are frustrated if a business that they want to buy from isn't available online. Consumers prefer to buy from businesses that have an established online profile. Too many businesses don't develop their online presence and only present a static, post-card version of a website instead of the required e-commerce site.

By the year 2021, Irish consumers will spend €14.1 billion a year online, but more than half of that may go to retailers outside the country, according to the Virgin Media Digital Insights Report January 2018. Irish SMEs that do not engage in digital marketing are likely to miss out.

This new era in digital marketing is like a second revolution: the first saw the arrival of digital marketing; the second is honing to be more personalised, consumer-friendly and focussed on building customer loyalty. You have the opportunity to make the online experience for your customers a wonderful one. Get deep customer insights. Individualise the customer. Use analytics to track their behaviour, to understand them better and to give them what they need. Develop long-term relationships with your online audience and provide an online experience that provides the right information to consumers at the moment they request it, fostering loyal advocates for your business.

How this book will help you

This is a short book. Its primary aim is to simplify digital marketing for busy people. I use case studies, insights, and the latest thinking to help you understand digital marketing and attract customers online.

Most businesses today are challenged by the power of the consumer. Most customers want to be able to complete their purchase online. Consumers demand a lot: efficient technology, secure systems, accurate images and reliable description – preferably on video.

Consumers also have the right and power to reject digital marketing by ad-blocking, spam filters and unsubscribing.

In this book, I wanted to address the concerns faced by all businesses, including professional firms, in deciding on the right digital marketing channels, e-commerce options and content. My aim is to demystify digital marketing and assist you in creating a simpler, happier, more engaging and innovative online presence for your customers.

CHAPTER ONE
CUSTOMER INSIGHTS

1

"Customers don't just want to buy; they want to experience. Customers are no longer satisfied by timely delivery, perfect product and expectations that are satisfied. In online marketing, you have to deliver more. You have to deliver a user experience that makes customers happy."

TONY HSIEH, DELIVERING HAPPINESS: A PATH TO PASSION, PROFITS AND PURPOSE (2012)

If you want to succeed in the digital marketing world, begin with the customer. This chapter is about keeping your customers close and your online customers even closer, getting to know them really well.

Getting customer insights

'Customer insights' is an umbrella term used to describe the process of researching the needs, motivations and desires of customers. Used in this context, the main aim is to gather enough information to help you to deliver services, products, experiences and online content that customers would like but are not already getting. In theory, if you produce the content that your ideal customer wants, then they should be able to find their way to you online.

Customer insights research is a powerful tool. Insights can help you to avoid bombarding customers with unnecessary noise and help to stimulate content that calms, reassures and inspires customer loyalty. In short – it's revolutionary.

Fáilte Ireland
Fáilte Ireland – the Irish Tourist Board – has successfully used customer insights to create a unique package for tourists. Fáilte Ireland uses customer insights extensively to understand the motivations and requirements of global and Irish holiday-makers.

CASE STUDY WILD ATLANTIC WAY — Prior to 2013, Fáilte Ireland had a problem with the marketing of Ireland. To international tourists, Ireland was perceived as a green and friendly place that they would visit 'someday'.

At the same time, the Irish tourist industry was on its knees – down €1 billion in revenue due to the global recession. The challenge was to package Ireland into a number of distinct regions to meet the needs and desires of tourists from all over the globe. From that, the Wild Atlantic Way was conceived, 'Ireland's first long-distance touring route, stretching along the Atlantic coast from Donegal to West Cork'.

Fáilte Ireland conducted research to understand emerging trends in the international tourism industry, which included global growth in tourism, the aging population, globalisation and the emergence of the large millennial market segment (aged 18 to 34). The team came up with a global segmentation model that divided international tourists into seven marketable segments reflected in seven distinct personas: Great Escapers, Social Energisers, Culturally Curious, Top Tenners, Nature Lovers, Spoil Us and Easy-going Socialisers. Three segments were selected as ideal. The Great Escapers market segment was deemed the best fit overall for marketing the Wild Atlantic Way.

The website, wildatlanticway.com, provides the Great Escapers with a variety of tools to help them research and plan their escape holiday experience in Ireland including:

- Trip Planner – a route planning function.
- Explore the Route – a geo-map to identify local attractions along your route, with information on cultural events, heritage locations and historical sites.
- Share your Experience – a user-generated content application. This allows Great Escaper tourists to share their holiday experiences.

With the priority customer segment in mind, the marketing of the Wild Atlantic Way is supported by social media, video, traditional advertising and a stellar website. Source: Fáilte Ireland.

Spotting the trends

Like the Wild Atlantic Way consumer insights programme, you also need to map your consumer journey, identify market trends and segment your market.

Map your consumer journey

Write out the journey that the consumers of your product or service take. **Figure 1.1** below summarises the work that Fáilte Ireland did. Note how they go back as far as the stimulus that triggered the customers' desire to go on holiday.

FIGURE 1.1 — WILD ATLANTIC WAY – THE CUSTOMER JOURNEY (SOURCE: FÁILTE IRELAND)

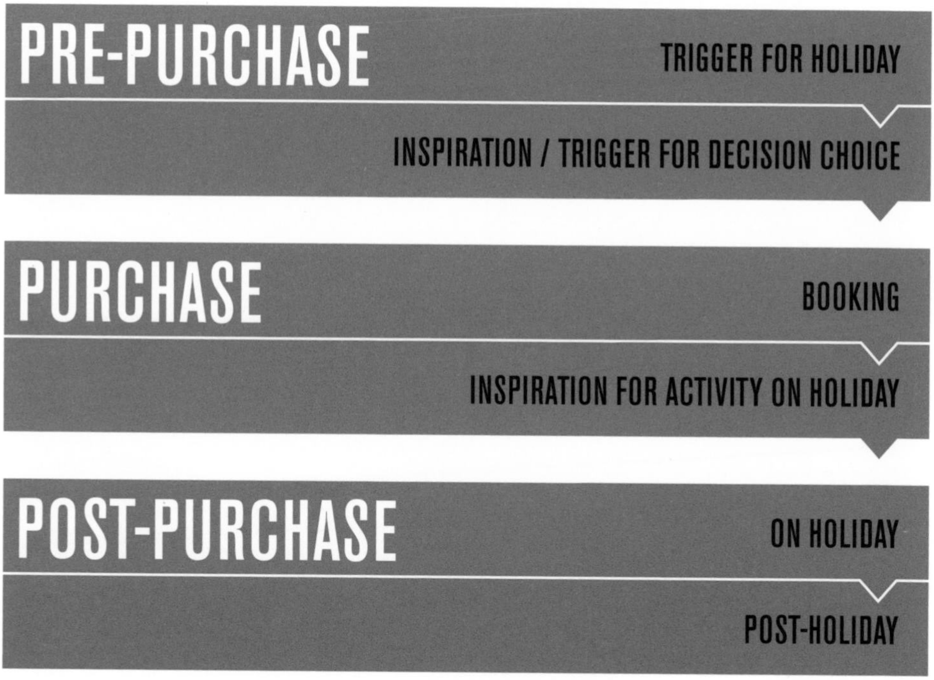

PRE-PURCHASE

TRIGGER FOR HOLIDAY

INSPIRATION / TRIGGER FOR DECISION CHOICE

PURCHASE

BOOKING

INSPIRATION FOR ACTIVITY ON HOLIDAY

POST-PURCHASE

ON HOLIDAY

POST-HOLIDAY

This straightforward exercise helps to identify each step that customers take when they are considering a purchase. Following this path will help you supply the right information to your customer's information source – and that might be via a blog or news article, a particular website, or social media sites like Facebook.

Identify market trends

When you first set up a business, you're very mindful of current and near-future market trends. As business picks up, you're less likely to look at strategic trends. Yet, they are ever-changing and vital to stay in touch with.

With the segmentation model for the Wild Atlantic Way, the Fáilte Ireland team really focused on global market trends and looked at evolving themes worldwide, including smartphone usage, what inspires leisure travel and the growing interest in 'intangible heritage'.

Segment your market

Segmentation is as simple as dividing your customers into groups with similar needs, motivation and characteristics. Today, segmentation focuses more on the motivation of consumers rather than their demographics. If you understand what motivates your best customers – learning, exploring, escaping, luxury, friendships, for example – you can design the right digital content strategy to attract their attention. In focusing on content that meets customers' motivations, you are genuinely appealing to them as people.

Grouping customers into segments also allows for economies of scale in buying media and producing content and helps you to deliver more targeted, less scattered marketing messages.

GREAT ESCAPERS

CULTURALLY CURIOUS

SOCIAL ENERGISERS

MARKET SEGMENTS

TOP TENNERS

NATURE LOVERS

SPOIL US

EASY-GOING SOCIALISERS

Fáilte Ireland segmented consumers into seven groups and then chose three priority market segments for their international tourism marketing drive (see **Figure 1.2**). Prioritisation of segments can lend simplicity and clarity to your digital marketing drive. Your target segments tend to be the types of customers that your business finds most profitable and most loyal. Can you identify your prime market segments? It is best to select sub-segments that are most suitable for your business and concentrate your efforts on getting to know them and appealing to their needs and desires. The Wild Atlantic Way team chose Great Escapers, Social Energisers and the Culturally Curious seg-ments, which they estimated added up to 145 million potential tourists from four key markets: Great Britain, the US, Germany and France.

Attracting the right customers to your business

Within a short time of launch, the Wild Atlantic Way digital team won a number of accolades for their digital marketing. How can you produce a digital marketing plan and suite to rival professionals like the Wild Atlantic Way team? You are probably on a budget, both from time and money per-spectives. The Fáilte Ireland case shows how

FIGURE 1.2 — WILD ATLANTIC WAY – GLOBAL SEGMENTATION MODEL (SOURCE: FÁILTE IRELAND)

SEGMENTS SELECTED

| SOCIAL ENERGISERS | CULTURALLY CURIOUS | GREAT ESCAPERS |

to investigate your customers' motivations, needs, trends, segments and their mind-set. If you use these tools, then your digital marketing has a much better chance of succeeding. Remember, you want to build a community of loyal advocates for your brand and those advocates will come from your most profitable market segments.

Figure 1.3 on page 10 shows eight ways to extract customer insights so that you maximise your digital marketing resources and attract the right leads to your business. Ultimately, your aim is to generate leads – a deep understanding of the motivations of customers is the best place to start.

FIGURE 1.3 — EIGHT WAYS TO ATTRACT THE RIGHT CUSTOMERS TO YOUR BUSINESS

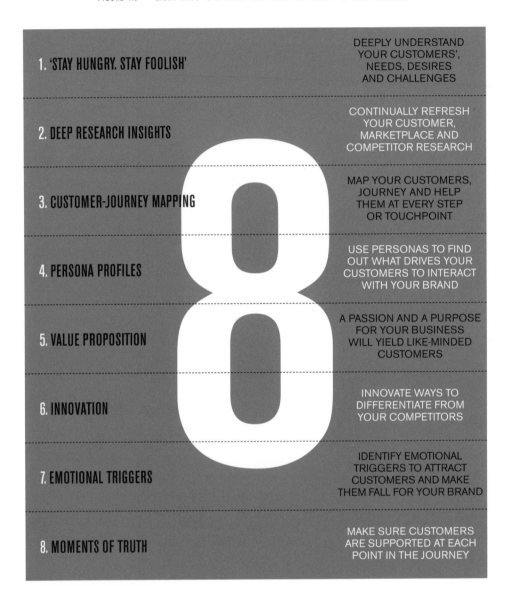

1. 'STAY HUNGRY. STAY FOOLISH'	DEEPLY UNDERSTAND YOUR CUSTOMERS', NEEDS, DESIRES AND CHALLENGES
2. DEEP RESEARCH INSIGHTS	CONTINUALLY REFRESH YOUR CUSTOMER, MARKETPLACE AND COMPETITOR RESEARCH
3. CUSTOMER-JOURNEY MAPPING	MAP YOUR CUSTOMERS, JOURNEY AND HELP THEM AT EVERY STEP OR TOUCHPOINT
4. PERSONA PROFILES	USE PERSONAS TO FIND OUT WHAT DRIVES YOUR CUSTOMERS TO INTERACT WITH YOUR BRAND
5. VALUE PROPOSITION	A PASSION AND A PURPOSE FOR YOUR BUSINESS WILL YIELD LIKE-MINDED CUSTOMERS
6. INNOVATION	INNOVATE WAYS TO DIFFERENTIATE FROM YOUR COMPETITORS
7. EMOTIONAL TRIGGERS	IDENTIFY EMOTIONAL TRIGGERS TO ATTRACT CUSTOMERS AND MAKE THEM FALL FOR YOUR BRAND
8. MOMENTS OF TRUTH	MAKE SURE CUSTOMERS ARE SUPPORTED AT EACH POINT IN THE JOURNEY

1. 'Stay hungry. Stay foolish'

You should never take your customers for granted. Stay hungry for new business development ideas and new ways to make life better for your customers. Stay foolish and never assume that you know everything about your customers.

"Stay hungry. Stay foolish." STEVE JOBS

2. Deep research insights

Market research can be done in a number of ways, including: focus group interviews, online surveys, recording customer feedback, website and social media analytics, in-store behaviour or face-to-face conversations. A combination of some or all of these can yield answers.

It's also important to understand the characteristics and behaviour of people within your market segments and the types emerging with online spending power. One of the most powerful and fastest growing consumer groups is millennials (see **Figure** 1.4). Look at your target market and work out which generation they fit into.

FIGURE 1.4 — FIVE KEY THINGS TO KNOW ABOUT MILLENNIALS (SOURCE: FÁILTE IRELAND)

FIVE KEY THINGS TO KNOW ABOUT MILLENNIALS

Millennials (aged 18 to 34) make up 1.8 billion out of the 7 billion total global population.

Millennials are driven by FOMO – 'fear of missing out'.

Millennials' prioritise experiences over other purchases; their travel spending often outpaces spending on other items.

98% of millennials own and use a smart-phone on a daily basis.

By 2020 this market will be taking 47% more international trips than 2013, with many young travellers looking for:

• unique and authentic experiences

• companies that listen to their feedback

• opportunities to learn something new

• word of mouth recommendations.

3. Customer journey mapping

Customer 'touch points' are your brand's points of contact with your customers, before, during and after they make a purchase. They are not always obvious and may span quite diverse areas of your business. Some of your touch points, such as your distribution and delivery service, may not even be easily controlled by you, but they do impact on your business and make an impression on your customer.

There are touch points at which your potential customer is only surfing, researching and comparing notes about you and your competitors and points at which the sale actually happens. In customer-journey mapping, you have to provide the right level of information to satisfy each need of the customer when it is required. For example, you may have top-class in-store service, but if your website is difficult to navigate, then the customer experience becomes negative. You have to find a way of making all touch points a sales opportunity.

The 7 x 7 Customer Journey Touch Points Matrix in **Figure 1.5** will help you to organise your product/service information for each point of the customer's journey. It's up to you to map out that customer journey and create excellent scenarios for the customer.

Figure 1.5 is an example of how to work your 7 x 7 Matrix to your best advantage. If you run a small hotel along the Wild Atlantic Way, how do you attract customers during their customer journey? Under **Pre-purchase /Brand awareness** promote your brand by writing blog posts about your area, the local amenities, and useful articles such as "Best places to have a picnic along the route".

Under **Pre-purchase/Research** use your website to provide the information that your best customers might want, e.g. of: local heritage sites; sports facilities, e.g. golf courses, horse riding stables; local restaurants; etc.

For **Purchase/Customer Service** make sure that your website is easy to navigate for booking. Respond to any queries quickly. Provide an 'out-of-hours' call-back service to answer questions.

Your job is to follow the process or path that your customer takes and ensure that you are supporting them every step of the way.

FIGURE 1.5 — THE CUSTOMER JOURNEY 7 x 7 TOUCH POINTS MATRIX

		PRE-PURCHASE			PURCHASE		POST-PURCHASE	
		Brand Awareness	Research	Pricing	Customer Service	Sale	Delivery	Queries
CUSTOMER	Brand Promotion	Blog articles on local history, amenities, heritage sites and points of interest.	List useful information: local amenities, details of restaurants, heritage sites, interesting stores.					
	Online Ads and Social Media							
	Word of Mouth							
	Website		Attractive website; useful content; images to show best features of the hotel and the local area.		Make sure booking easy to navigate; respond to queries quickly using a live chat feature; provide out of hours assistance.			
	Email							
	Contact by Phone							
	Physical Store						Welcoming and familiar approach; innovative touches, such as homemade produce; friendly environment.	

4. Customer persona profiles

The use of customer persona profiles can help you move from general to more relevant and targeted communication online. Where possible, use existing customer data to inform your persona profiles. You should aim to create between three and five personas – the three main steps for doing so are outlined in **Figure** 1.6:

FIGURE 1.6 — STEPS TO CREATING CUSTOMER PERSONAS

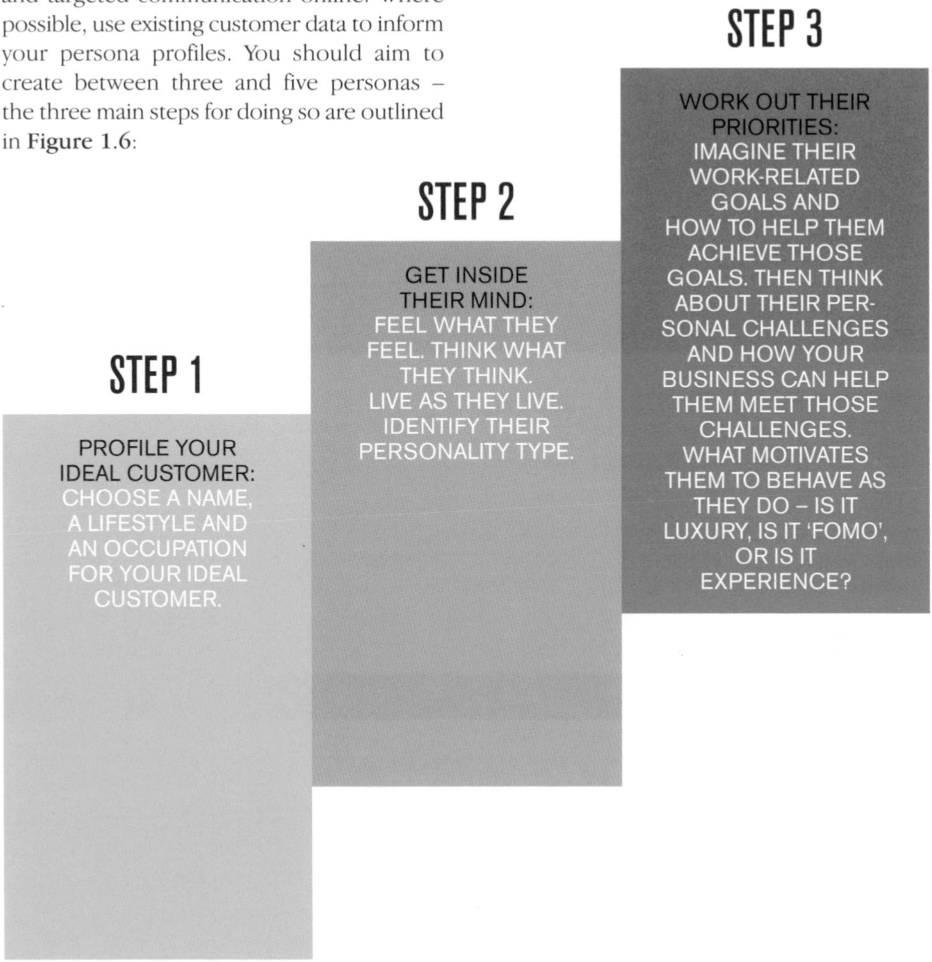

STEP 3

WORK OUT THEIR PRIORITIES: IMAGINE THEIR WORK-RELATED GOALS AND HOW TO HELP THEM ACHIEVE THOSE GOALS. THEN THINK ABOUT THEIR PERSONAL CHALLENGES AND HOW YOUR BUSINESS CAN HELP THEM MEET THOSE CHALLENGES. WHAT MOTIVATES THEM TO BEHAVE AS THEY DO – IS IT LUXURY, IS IT 'FOMO', OR IS IT EXPERIENCE?

STEP 2

GET INSIDE THEIR MIND: FEEL WHAT THEY FEEL. THINK WHAT THEY THINK. LIVE AS THEY LIVE. IDENTIFY THEIR PERSONALITY TYPE.

STEP 1

PROFILE YOUR IDEAL CUSTOMER: CHOOSE A NAME, A LIFESTYLE AND AN OCCUPATION FOR YOUR IDEAL CUSTOMER.

Building personas can help make you more useful in addressing your customers' particular needs and solving their problems. Focusing on your customers' needs and goals makes understanding and exceeding their expectations easier. You move from being a seller to a supporter, which is more effective for your customer and more satisfying for you.

In the Wild Atlantic Way persona example in **Figure** 1.7, note the close scrutiny that John Gills, a typical Great Escaper consumer, receives – how he has an occupation, interests and specific sources of information. Doesn't this level of detail really make you feel that you could communicate with John Gills? That's the value of persona profiles – they can imaginatively transform segments or groups of similar customers into human beings.

5. Value proposition

Your values will underpin the overall personality of your business, as will your value proposition. Your value proposition is the value you provide to your customers for the money that they are prepared to give you in return. When you know what motivates

FIGURE 1.7 — WILD ATLANTIC WAY PERSONA: GREAT ESCAPER — UK
(SOURCE: FÁILTE IRELAND – WWW.FAILTEIRELAND.IE/INTERNATIONAL-SALES/
INTERNATIONAL-SALES/GREAT-ESCAPERS/GREAT-ESCAPER-PERSONAS.ASPX)

NAME: JOHN GILLS	AGE: 32	PROFESSION: PARAMEDIC

John works as a paramedic with an ambulance service in the North East of England – stress is part of his daily working life. To help de-stress, he runs three to four times a week with his local running club, Tyne Bridge Harriers, and aims to complete a half marathon/marathon every year – the Great North Run is his favourite.

A yogi, he subscribes to Yogagio, watching 'how to' videos so he can cram in a yoga session at home. He also follows a number of health and lifestyle sites like MindBodyGreen and Elephant Journal for daily positive pep-ups.

As an NHS employee, his salary doesn't allow an overly extravagant lifestyle, so he subscribes to daily emails from deal platforms like Groupon, Wowcher and Actica.

Interest / Hobbies	Barriers to Visiting	Digital Interest Touch Points	Digital Travel Touch Points
• Running • Mountain biking • Health food • Yoga • TV shows: House of Cards, Game of Thrones	Believes Ireland is expensive, particularly when it comes to dining out Limited time is a factor; with a busy work schedule, his usual escapes are within close proximity to home Unaware of diverse outdoor activities on offer in Ireland	The Independent The Observer The Times Netflix Yogagio MindBodyGreen Elephant Journal Facebook Instagram	Lastminute.com BBC Travel Travel Zoo SecretEscape Guardian Travel TheJournal.co.uk The Sunday Times

IMPLICATIONS

Content that appeals to John needs to communicate speed and ease of access to a variety of activities close to airport hubs. Although he likes to connect with nature, he also likes to post #latergrams of his adventures on Instagram and Facebook. Working every second weekend, his travel go-tos are supplement and lifestyle sites. He likes information in digestible formats, such as top 10 lists, which he often sticks on the fridge. Visual content that shows breath-taking landscapes are a key travel motivator. Mobile is a key channel for him to access content.

your customer segments and you have created persona profiles of ideal customers, designing a value proposition to suit those particular people becomes less daunting.

Of course, what people perceive as 'value' is relative and personal to them. Customers make their purchase decisions based on their perception of the value of your product/service. You need to figure out what they value most, their priorities, and aim to always meet their highest priorities.

6. Innovation

Building on your value proposition, innovations are the differentiating factors that will enable your business to outshine others. The businesses that stand out online manage to identify something that differentiates them from competitors – an element that has impact, makes sense and addresses customers' needs. **Figure 1.8** outlines three types of innovation that can help you to be different online.

FIGURE 1.8 — THREE TYPES OF INNOVATION

INCREMENTAL INNOVATION

1

In a December 2007 article for the *Harvard Business Review*, George S. Day, Professor of Marketing at the Wharton School in the University of Pennsylvania, describes two types of innovation: incremental innovation, which he calls 'small I'; and the risky, big projects and market-changing innovations, new to the company and new to the world, which he calls 'big I'.

Differentiation comes from knowing your product, customers and competitors intimately. Great impact comes from selling what you are really good at to people who really want what you offer. Day describes how you can make small incremental changes to stand out. Toothpaste brands do this effectively by marketing added ingredients that 'prevent cavities' or 'whiten teeth'.

MARKET-CHANGING INNOVATION

2

PROMOTIONAL INNOVATION

3

It's a challenge for any business to be different from its competitors. In their book, *Blue Ocean Strategy: How to create uncontested market space and make the competition irrelevant* (2005), Reneé Mauborgne and W. Chan Kim advocate the 'blue water strategy' – finding an entirely different business offering that steps completely away from the competition. The arrival of online shopping to replace mail order catalogues was one such market-changing innovation.

Promotional innovation includes how you repackage and market an existing product or service. It may be a promotional offer, discount code, voucher, free trial or an invitation to find out more. If you adopt deal-based promotions, be careful not to undermine the long-term viability of your business.

Another form of promotional innovation is to repackage or represent a product/service and offer better value to consumers – an award-winning example is webdoctor.ie.

7. Emotional triggers

It's important to consider the emotions of the buyer when you are designing your digital marketing campaign. Customers can act on the basis of their emotions; many purchases are governed primarily by wants, not needs.

Your work on personas will help to uncover the emotional aspect of your buyer – the human side. Sometimes businesses using digital marketing fail to reflect on the emotional side of their customers.

Emotionally, people find it hard to stand up to being invaded, bombarded and assaulted with information. It's one of the emotional difficulties that human beings have to face today – an overload of information and stimulus. If you consider your customer's emotions carefully, you will find yourself creating an oasis of calm and clarity online for your customers, as outlined in **Figure 1.9**, by being brief, clear, concise and relevant, providing excellent service, offering surprise rewards and building trust and loyalty.

FIGURE 1.9 — HOW TO MAKE LIFE EASY FOR YOUR CUSTOMERS ONLINE

BE BRIEF

KEEP YOUR MESSAGE AND INFORMATION BRIEF, TO THE POINT AND EASY TO ACCESS. USE BULLET POINTS, IMAGES, VIDEO, AND CHARTS TO CONVEY YOUR MESSAGE.

BE RELEVANT

RESEARCH YOUR CUSTOMERS' REQUIREMENTS AND APPEAL TO WHAT THEY REALLY NEED, THEN FIND WAYS TO ENTERTAIN, AMUSE AND ENTHRAL THEM. ALWAYS APPEAL TO WHAT YOU KNOW THEY LIKE, WHAT THEY WANT.

PROVIDE STELLAR SERVICE

MAKE SURE THAT YOU SUPPORT SALES WITH STELLAR SERVICE. IF CUSTOMERS ENCOUNTER BAD SERVICE, THEY WILL NOT RETURN AND THEY COULD WARN OFF MANY OTHER, POTENTIAL CUSTOMERS.

Don't underestimate the power of emotional connections when marketing your business online. The content that you use should include stories, journeys, images, music and testimonials that evoke an emotional connection.

"We design our website to have the appearance of an old-fashioned general store, while featuring merchandise that will make the customer's life easier and a bit happier."

LILLIAN VERNON — FOUNDER OF THE MULTI-MILLION DOLLAR, US ONLINE RETAILER LILLIANVERNON.COM

BE CLEAR AND CONCISE

WHEN WRITING FOR THE WEB OR ANY OTHER FORM OF MARKETING, AVOID COMPLICATED LANGUAGE. MAKE YOUR LANGUAGE SIMPLE, ACCESSIBLE AND EASY TO RELATE TO.

OFFER SURPRISE REWARDS

PEOPLE LIKE SURPRISES AND REWARDS. A VOUCHER TOWARDS THE NEXT PURCHASE, A FREE GIFT, FASTER SHIPPING, OR ANY OTHER REWARD FOR LOYALTY. NO MATTER HOW MUCH PEOPLE HAVE, THEY STILL ENJOY A SURPRISE.

BUILD TRUST

IT TAKES TIME TO BUILD TRUST BUT ONCE THE RELATIONSHIP IS ESTABLISHED, YOU HAVE A CHANCE OF HOLDING ON TO LOYAL CUSTOMERS. TRUST INVOLVES RESPONSIBLE SERVICE, POSITIVE INTERACTION AND GOODWILL. TO BUILD TRUST, YOU DON'T HAVE TO BE PERFECT, BUT YOU DO HAVE TO BE CREDIBLE, RESPONSIVE AND READY TO GO THE EXTRA MILE.

8. Moments of truth

Organisations like Fáilte Ireland spend time refining how they present their offering to their customers and potential customers. They work along the customer journey to ensure that at each critical touch point, customers are supported and helped, and that the process is simplified.

It is at these critical moments of truth along the touch-point curve that you can lose customers if you don't make the process easy to follow and intuitive. Moments of truth are individual to each business and as you work your way through the customer journey, you will have to identify yours.

Keep in mind, however, that your customers want you to make their life easier – easily contactable, easy website navigation, clearly defined options, and clear product visuals – so that they don't have to work too hard. Customers also want faster delivery, easy ordering, straightforward purchase processing and kind and thoughtful customer service. Don't just compare your service to your sector or industry peers: aim to be the best by looking at what is possible across the online spectrum.

Remember: though segmenting is important, ultimately you are communicating with individuals, not groups, so address them as individuals.

AT A GLANCE   CHAPTER ONE

The Wild Atlantic Way case study gives us a good sense of how to individualise the customer. Fáilte Ireland show us how to gain deep insights into the behaviour of our ideal customers as well as grouping those ideal customers into segments. Their personas illustrates the motivations of the 'Great Escapers'.

Use these kinds of tools for your business and you will know your best customers as individuals – so you can help them on their purchase journey. You will know where they hang out. What motivates them. What forms of communication they rely on. You will know your customers intimately and so you can provide an oasis of calm, relevant and reassuring information.

Plotting the customer journey is a valuable experience. We have looked at the journey as involving three steps – pre-purchase, purchase and post-purchase – to gain a deeper understanding of what is required to support customers online at each touch point, at each step of the journey.

Once you understand the customer, their journey and the touch points they are likely to encounter, then you can begin to use innovations to 'wow' your customer. Small, incremental innovations that attract customers, such as vouchers, partner deals, local insights, entertaining stories, friendly notes and out-of-hours assistance. Get your team involved in finding more interesting ways to create warm customer relationships.

These insights help considerably in the process of lead generation. You want to attract more business online. Good communication will get you leads.

CHAPTER TWO
CONTENT

2

Search engine results pages (SERPs) are web pages served to users when they search for something online using a search engine, such as Google. The user enters their search query (often using specific terms and phrases known as keywords), upon which the search engine presents them with a SERP. Source: wordstream.com.

What is 'content'?

Content is the information, entertainment, guidance and support that you provide online for your target market segments in order to entice them to stay and look around. It should be produced with specific customer personas in mind. Content may take the form of website text, blogs, newsletters, social media posts, white papers, images, videos, games and other interactive material (This chapter focuses on free content. **Chapter 5** covers paid results and the realm of online advertising.).

Content works in a number of ways to help promote your brand. First, if the content is relevant, entertaining or useful to consumers, they will read it. Secondly, if your content is well read and appreciated by consumers, search engines such as Google will see that it is good content. This will boost your ranking on search engine results pages (SERPs). Look at Titanicbelfast.com for inspiration.

SERPs are web pages served to users when they search for something online using a search engine, such as Google. The user enters their search query using keywords and the search engine presents them with a results page. SERPs are also based on a wide range of factors such as the person's location, browsing history and social media interactions. How SERPs appear changes regularly as search engine providers are constantly working to hone the results to meet the needs of users in order to provide a more intuitive experience.

SERPs typically contain two types of content – **organic results** and **paid results**.

ORGANIC RESULTS are listings of web pages that appear as a result of the search engine's algorithm. The more relevant, appreciated and entertaining your content, the more likely you are to rank highly in organic search engine results.

PAID RESULTS are the advertisements, often denoted by the word 'ad', that appear at the top, bottom and sides of a SERP. These results appear when an advertiser has paid for certain keywords.

CASE STUDY BLUE SEPTEMBER — Blue September is an annual campaign designed to raise awareness of cancer in men and fundraise for men's health programmes under Men's Cancer Alliance, an umbrella alliance formed by the Mater Hospital Foundation, the Mercy Hospital Foundation and Cancer Care West, originally sponsored by VHI Healthcare.

The Blue September campaign set out to radically change men's reticence when it comes to their health. Research shows that men avoid dealing with health issues, often ignoring symptoms until they are forced to do something about them. VHI and the Men's Cancer Alliance found a fun and radical way to deliver a serious message about facing up to cancer.

In **Chapter 1**, we saw how to identify and target your customers or audience. The Blue September team was very clear that they were targeting men between the ages of 18 and 40. The mind-set and lifestyle of this audience was carefully researched in order to maximise the impact of the campaign.

The Blue September campaign runs annually over the course of a month using a mix of digital media, including social media, gaming, information guides, digital display and traditional media such as TV, press, cinema, radio and outdoor activities.

This campaign is an excellent illustration of how a multi-channel campaign, harnessing both digital and traditional media, can help to change hearts and minds in the sensitive area of men's health.

"With content marketing, the message is the virus, the carriers are your audience and a strong emotional connection to the message is the catalyst."

SOCIAL MEDIA TODAY, 15 NOVEMBER 2012

There are three lessons that we can derive from this sensitive and successful campaign:

- The campaign had to be 'high impact' to achieve the goals set out by the team.

- The team's 'game-changing' attitude that encouraged their male audience to take action.

- The third key element of the Blue September campaign is the integrated approach: they used a healthy mix of traditional and digital communication to attract their audience and to build the brand. Look at a variety of options when delivering your campaigns.

BLUE SEPTEMBER

HIGH IMPACT   GAME CHANGING   INTEGRATED APPROACH

High impact

You achieve high impact when you develop content that surprises your audience and evokes an emotional response from them. In **Chapter 1** we saw how researching what priority customers want and how they are motivated helps to focus the mind on providing information where it's needed along the customer journey. If you understand and individualise your customers, then you can find ways to really excite them along that journey.

Game changing

Content that becomes viral is not content that is just satisfactory, it is of real relevance and interest to the people it is designed for. High-impact digital marketing has to be emotionally engaging, deliver a message worth sharing and give the person reading it an alternative, insightful perspective.

The Blue September campaign harnesses celebrities, uses mobile phone apps, and a very simple concept to change the hearts and minds of men at risk of cancer. Simplicity is important. Most game-changing ideas are not complicated.

Game-changing digital marketing also gives you the option to use a variety of digital marketing assets, such as mobile apps, YouTube video, gaming and advanced social media pages. Using one or two of these methods can give you the impetus you need.

Game-changing digital marketing is both unique and powerful. If you can create game-changing services, websites, and other ways of communicating to your customers, you take the first step towards the marketing gold mine. Here are some great examples of game-changing digital work:

WILDATLANTICWAY.COM 'Explore the Route' feature.

TEDTALKS.COM Brilliant communication formula.

MICKSGARAGE.COM Car parts matching system.

The bottom line is this: identify the key deliverables that will impress customers and create a digital proposition – be it information, technology or service – that will make them loyal to your business.

Integrated approach

One of the biggest issues for many businesses all over the world is 'silo thinking'. This happens when teams are not working together for the good of the organisation. It happens in big businesses and it happens in small businesses. Silo thinking can also happen in marketing. An advertisement appears in a newspaper with entirely different branding and message from that of the business's website. A sales person talks about features and product capabilities that aren't backed up by the messages on their product's website.

Budgets stretch far further when marketing is fully integrated, which means that everyone across the organisation follows the same communication principles about the brand. It makes life easier for the customer too. The message that they get in-store, reflects the information they read on the website and is supported by the advertisement they came across in the newspaper.

The team that created the Blue September campaign wisely used a wide variety of media, including traditional and online advertising, gaming, and fact sheets, all reflecting the same clear messages. This created an impactful and more memorable campaign.

Figure 2.1 lists eight ideas and initiatives for you to consider in generating content for your consumers and using it to attract them or drive them to your business.

Using Content to Drive Traffic to Your Business

The new buzzword in digital marketing is 'humanise'. Remember that the customer is human and has needs. There are a few important methods you can use to fulfill your customer's specific needs.

FIGURE 2.1 — EIGHT WAYS TO USE CONTENT TO DRIVE
TRAFFIC TO YOUR BUSINESS

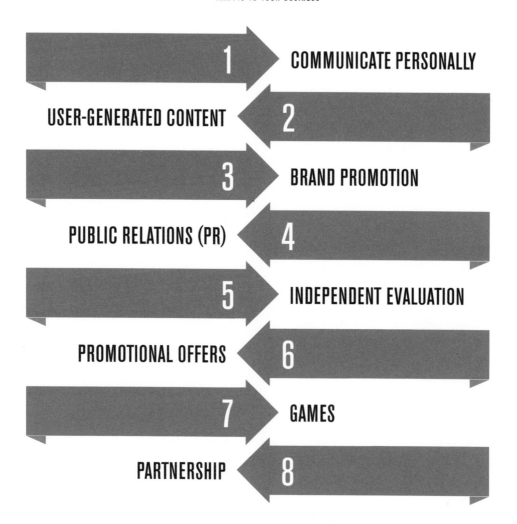

1 COMMUNICATE PERSONALLY

USER-GENERATED CONTENT 2

3 BRAND PROMOTION

PUBLIC RELATIONS (PR) 4

5 INDEPENDENT EVALUATION

PROMOTIONAL OFFERS 6

7 GAMES

PARTNERSHIP 8

1. Communicate personally

You have done your research and you know who your customers are or should be. Making an impact on these specific individuals requires a style of communication that makes them feel part of your brand and family of followers. One of the most impactful tools in digital marketing is to speak to people online as if they are in front of you. Take your communications from the general to the personal. If you don't buy into the human side of your customer, they won't buy into you.

For example, below is an email from online retailer Boden.co.uk to a first-time customer:

Dear Mary-Ann,

Thanks for placing an order with us. You've made us happier than all our favourite things: tea, dogs, crumpets and bank holidays.

We'll aim to deliver your goodies soon, but in the meantime, here's your order info.

Johnnie Boden

"Another common trap that many marketers fall into is focusing too much on trying to figure out how to generate a lot of buzz, when really they should be focused on building engagement and trust."

TONY HSIEH, DELIVERING HAPPINESS (2010)

2. User-generated content

One of the most valuable sources of content is – perhaps surprisingly – your customers. User-generated content (UGC) is a superb way to promote the value of your business because that promotion comes straight from the customer. This is a more trustworthy endorsement than information coming from the enterprise, which clearly has a vested interested. Research shows that consumers trust UGC more than other forms of media.

Customers' images, videos and testimonials are very powerful and compelling types of content that you can repackage and incorporate into your future marketing.

CASE STUDY CROWD-SOURCING CONTENT: THE SUGRU GALLERY — Sugru manufactures a soft substance that can be used to mend almost anything. Sugru customers enjoy sharing how they use Sugru to mend and remodel the most unusual domestic items and Sugru thereby crowd-sources UGC.

"Share your story. Tell us about your project. What problem did you fix? Why Sugru was great for the job? How did you apply it? Did it save you money, time, or both?

Did it earn you a bit of love? How did it make you feel? Hearing your stories gives us a special kind of joy. So please, don't spare us any details!" Source: https://sugru.com/upload

HOW TO INCREASE USER-GENERATED CONTENT

Invite your online followers to contribute their ideas, insights or images on your website or social media pages.

Offer a prize to encourage participation by your followers.

Encourage some fun where possible by asking customers to submit entertaining ideas about how they enjoyed your product or service.

3. Brand promotion

Brand promotion is the act of getting your brand out into the market. Your brand is critically important in attracting customers to your business. An attractive and well-recognised brand will have a much easier time in the digital world. It will be recognised by customers and search engines, and be more likely to receive attention from online communities.

Developing and establishing a brand may happen entirely online or you may wish to support the brand by using traditional media such as print and outdoor advertising. Integrated marketing involves applying a consistent brand image and message across the various media channels. A consistent look, feel and message greatly increases the impact and each promotional opportunity will reinforce the other.

Figure 2.2 (opposite) lists eight ways to drive traffic to your website using various brand promotions, including product information brochures, advertisements and even the name of the business itself.

4. Public Relations (PR)

Online PR is not entirely different to traditional PR, which in this context involves businesses gaining exposure to their customers using

FIGURE 2.2 — EIGHT WAYS TO DRIVE TRAFFIC TO YOUR WEB-
SITE USING AN INTEGRATED MEDIA APPROACH

MAKE THE NAME OF YOUR
BUSINESS YOUR WEBSITE
ADDRESS, FOR EXAMPLE:
123.IE OR TAXBACK.COM

INCLUDE YOUR WEBSITE AND
SOCIAL MEDIA PROFILES ON
ALL ADVERTISEMENTS

PUT YOUR WEBSITE ADDRESS
ON ALL PROMOTIONAL MATERIAL
SUCH AS BROCHURES
AND FLYERS

INCLUDE YOUR WEBSITE
ADDRESS ON ALL STATIONERY

WHEN SENDING INVITATIONS
TO EVENTS, INVITE PEOPLE TO
REGISTER THROUGH YOUR
WEBSITE OR ON FACEBOOK

INCLUDE YOUR WEBSITE AND
SOCIAL MEDIA PROFILES ON ALL
CUSTOMER CORRESPONDENCE,
INVOICES AND RECEIPTS

MAKE SURE THAT RELEVANT
INFORMATION ABOUT PRODUCTS
OR SERVICES IS ONLINE,
AND REFER PEOPLE TO YOUR
WEBSITE FOR MORE DETAILS

LIMIT THE INFORMATION GIVEN
ON BUSINESS CARDS OR
OTHER PROMOTIONAL
MATERIALS AND DIRECT PEOPLE
TO YOUR WEBSITE FOR
DETAILED INFORMATION

topics of public interest and news items that do not require direct payment. PR is a valuable tool for driving traffic and attracting attention to your business. The best thing about PR is that it's relatively low cost – great for your budget! If you know your audience, where they hang out online and what they read, then you can use PR to grab their attention.

However, there is some skill required for getting the right PR, which is why many businesses pay a professional PR agent. Your press release has to be newsworthy, interesting, topical and relevant to the publications that your prospective customers read. So, make sure your content is current and topical. Give it an eye-catching headline. Use interesting statistics, lively stories and customer journeys to produce an interesting press release that people will want to read and, more importantly, share.

When sending information to the media, remember that you are among thousands seeking free publicity. Journalists and bloggers are utterly bombarded with press releases and promo materials.

In my view, PR works best when you have a topic, information or story that is compelling. For example, local stories, featuring local people, working in partnership, are very good for getting local publicity.

Any PR you get is good for search engine optimisation. Search engines will rank you highly if you publish good PR articles regularly on your website and particularly if publications publish links to your website or social media pages online.

5. Independent evaluation

There is an old saying that 'self-praise is no praise'. The most prized praise for any business is a positive customer testimonial. Star ratings on Amazon, top scores on TripAdvisor, testimonials on WhatClinic.com all confirm that your business is a winning force.

In today's celebrity age, endorsements by well-known public figures are very effective. An example of this is how Blue September invited Bernard Whelan and Dermot O'Shea to support their campaign – Irish comedians with particular appeal to men in the target age group.

Of course, there is usually a cost involved in getting a celebrity to endorse your product. Most sports professionals, for example, charge endorsement fees that are not within the budgets of a small business. To get celebrity endorsement for your business for free requires time and patience, and maybe even a little cunning, but it can be done! In the **Introduction** I briefly mentioned how Niall Horan tweeted to the benefit of Funky Christmas Jumpers. Few marketers can approach celebrities directly. However, most celebrities have a team – PR people, personal assistants and other associates. If you have a new product or service, don't write to One Direction. Get in front of one of their team.

Figure 2.3 lists six ways to encourage others to publicise your brand credibly and independently verified.

FIGURE 2.3 — SIX WAYS TO GET INDEPENDENT EVALUATIONS

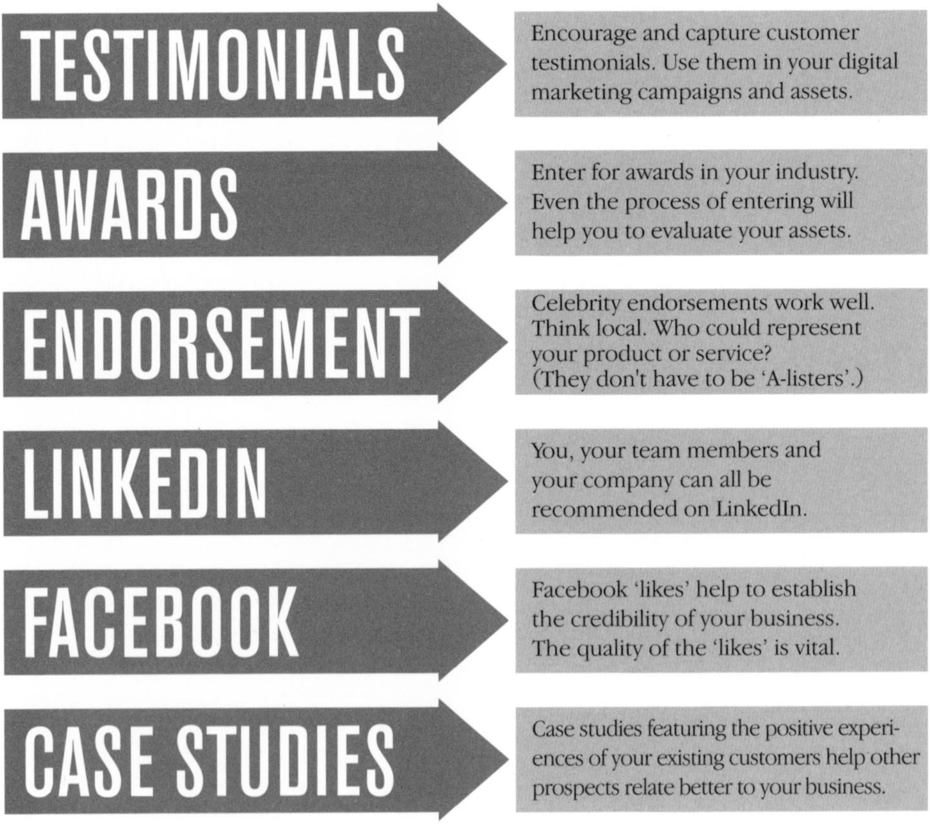

TESTIMONIALS
Encourage and capture customer testimonials. Use them in your digital marketing campaigns and assets.

AWARDS
Enter for awards in your industry. Even the process of entering will help you to evaluate your assets.

ENDORSEMENT
Celebrity endorsements work well. Think local. Who could represent your product or service? (They don't have to be 'A-listers'.)

LINKEDIN
You, your team members and your company can all be recommended on LinkedIn.

FACEBOOK
Facebook 'likes' help to establish the credibility of your business. The quality of the 'likes' is vital.

CASE STUDIES
Case studies featuring the positive experiences of your existing customers help other prospects relate better to your business.

6. Promotional offers

'Black Friday', 'Cyber Monday', January sales, mid-season reductions – in the retail business, discounts are used liberally to drive sales. However, tread carefully when offering goods and services at low prices. Your aim is to generate long-term, quality business and not once-off sales. At the same time, you have to find price-points and offers that fit with your business model. Find ways to attract attention that are not totally price-based and keep the longer term relationship with customers in mind. **Figure 2.4** shows some ideas on how to entice customers to your business.

FIGURE 2.4 — EIGHT ONLINE OFFERS TO ENGAGE YOUR CUSTOMERS

ENGAGE YOUR CUSTOMERS

WELCOME INTRODUCTORY OFFERS

- DISCOUNT CODES
- SALE PRICES
- COMPETITIONS
- GROUP BUYING SITES, e.g. Groupon, Livingsocial

THANK YOU FOR THE PURCHASE

- FREE DELIVERY
- FREE GIFT OR SAMPLE

BUY FROM US AGAIN

- DISCOUNT VOUCHER FOR NEXT PURCHASE
- LOYALTY SCHEME

7. Games

Gamification, or the use of online gaming, can be used to achieve specific commercial goals. Online games help people to interact with brands in a positive and entertaining way. The Blue September campaign offered an online, mobile-friendly game, 'Keepy Uppy', the object of which was to keep a virtual ball in the air as long as possible. Players could share their scores and invite others to play. After each session, a 'call-to-action' asked players to donate to the Men's Cancer Alliance. Well-executed gamification could help to build and reinforce your brand messages, as well as foster customer loyalty and regular interaction.

8. Partnership

Good partnerships generate great creativity and results. VHI teamed up with the Men's Cancer Alliance to create Blue September. No matter what business you are in, there are opportunities for online partnership. Small businesses can work very successfully with larger, non-conflicting businesses for a win–win result. Look around your local community. Is there a business or organisation that shares your values and approach to business with which could you share costs, ideas and digital marketing plans to help drive online business for each of you?

BONUS – SEVEN WAYS TO MAKE GOOD CONTENT

Shape your business to:

BE REAL

- Deliver what your customers want. McDonald's McCafé serves genuinely good coffee.
- Deliver a quality product or service. Ryanair flies all over Europe at a reasonable price with an excellent on-time record.
- Deliver as promised. Vanish does remove stains.
- Solve your customers' problems. Trivago endeavours to find the cheapest accommodation.

BE ICONIC

Stories have always held people spellbound. Fáilte Ireland has developed the story of Ireland's Ancient East as a way to illustrate the treasures of eastern Ireland to tourists.

BE FUNNY

Employ humour effectively in your digital marketing. Blendtec (see **Chapter 5**) uses humour successfully to market its high-powered blenders by blending everyday items such as mobile phones, even bricks. Well-placed humour can make your business more accessible, breaking down barriers, providing conversation opportunities and easing the relationship.

BE AWARE OF EMOTION

People are primarily emotional beings and it is key to remember this when you are communicating with customers. An online advertisement created by Banjoman Films for Home Store + More tells the story of a lonely older man who is waiting for his son and his family, living abroad, to come home to celebrate his retirement. Worth watching.

BE VISUAL

Develop a set of visuals that fit with your logo, brand and message. Images help to make navigating a website easier than reading chunks of text. But don't use too many images or the website could become cluttered and visitors put off. The images should reflect your customers' needs, not your desire to look grandiose, e.g. by using large photos of your building. It's important to always include good keywords in the image file name. (See thelittlemilkcompany.com for a good use of visuals.)

BE SIMPLE

Talk about what is important. Enough said.

BE KIND

How can your business fulfill an objective to be kind? Innocent Smoothies raise money for the charity Age Action every year by asking people to knit thousands of hats for smoothie bottles. The money goes to keep older people warm in the winter. 30 cents from every hatted bottle sold goes directly to Age Action. This simply kind and thoughtful campaign is charming and gains good PR.

AT A GLANCE   CHAPTER TWO

The best, most compelling content is user-generated content (UGC). UGC is also the most trusted form of content among consumers.

You need to provide the right platform for customer feedback and UGC feedback so that customers can easily upload their images, videos and stories. Social media (covered in more detail in **Chapter 4**) offers very convenient, cost-effective media for UGC. To kick start UGC, launch a campaign offering something valuable and ask people to tell their story about why they like your brand in return.

There are a number of other ways to generate good content:

• content partnerships with complementary businesses
• PR-attracting articles and news
• customer reviews and celebrity endorsement
• special offers and free online games.

A major part of content generation is scheduling. If you gather 15–30 pieces of content and then schedule them to run over a month, then you are more likely to succeed. A piece-meal, one-by-one approach is harder to sustain.

At the same time, always be on the lookout for representations of your brand to share on your website and social media pages. There are thousands of opportunities once you put that task on your agenda.

In South East Asia, there is a saying 'Same, same, but different.' This saying sums up the greatest difficulty for businesses transacting online today. There is so much competition that it is hard to stand out. By aiming for a high-impact approach, trying to up the game just a bit and approaching all your marketing in a harmonised and integrated way, you can move ahead.

CHAPTER THREE
YOUR WEBSITE

3

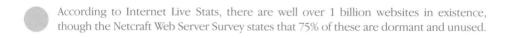

According to Internet Live Stats, there are well over 1 billion websites in existence, though the Netcraft Web Server Survey states that 75% of these are dormant and unused.

Your shop window to the world

Here is a question for you to consider: does your website stand out as excellent in terms of content, design and usefulness for the customer?

We discussed content and how to adapt your information to meet the needs of customers in the previous chapter. Websites need excellent content. They also need to be well-designed to attract and hold web-surfers. Most importantly, websites must address the needs of customers.

Websites are a great, largely untapped resource for entrepreneurs and the statistics prove this conclusively.

Your website is a shop window and modern consumers often base their purchase decisions on their perceptions of the online store. Consumers use websites as barometers for competence, capability and delivery.

• 59% of consumers said that if a business has no online presence, they would be less likely to do business with them in-store.
• 66% of consumers say that if a business has a poor online presence, they would be less likely to do business with it.

(SOURCE: DOT IE DIGITAL HEALTH INDEX — Q4 2017)

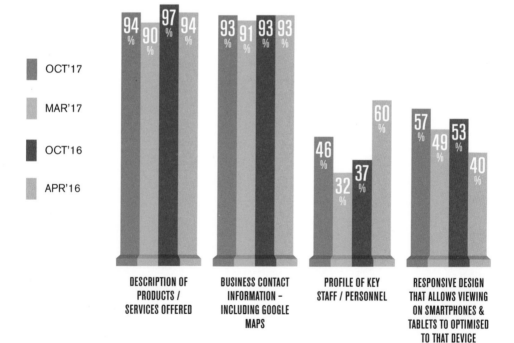

However, the vast majority of business websites have not received enough investment. They are 'postcard websites' carrying basic unchanging information about the company, its location and product or service descriptions. If you want to make an impact in your market, invest in your website. The age of the static, unchanging postcard website has gone. Customers want and expect much more.

So, what can you do to adapt to customer requirements? You want customers to find your website 'sticky' – in other words, when they land on your site, they don't leave straight away or bounce out of your site – they continue to browse your interesting content, images, videos, news, latest updates and articles. Your fresh ideas and special offers, the human stories around your products and services, will help to reduce the 'bounce rate' of your website, meaning that people will want to stick around longer.

Figure 3.1 below shows, according to research carried out by the Irish Research Domain Registry, the features and functionality available on the websites of Irish companies (or at least all companies that have a website in the first place!).

Figure 3.1 reveals a real opportunity for you to use your website to market your business and gain competitive advantage. Only a third of businesses use video. Only 34% can process payments online. Only 40% can take sales orders. Only 57% of websites can be viewed properly on devices such as smartphones and tablets. The websites of most Irish businesses still seem to be merely static 'postcards'. In 2017, significant improvements were recorded in the functionality that SMEs have placed on their websites. This is heartening, given the level of opportunity that abounds.

FIGURE 3.1 — HOW IRISH BUSINESSES CURRENTLY USE THEIR WEBSITES
(SOURCE: DOT IE DIGITAL HEALTH INDEX — Q4 2017)

VIDEO CONTENT | ABILITY TO BOOK / MAKE A RESERVATION | ABILITY TO TAKE SALES ORDERS | ABILITY TO PROCESS PAYMENTS | ABILITY FOR CUSTOMER TO SET UP PROFILES / USER ACCOUNTS

Here's how The Little Milk Company made a global impression with their web presence.

CASE STUDY THE LITTLE MILK COMPANY — Set up in 2008, the Little Milk Company comprises 10 family-run, organic dairy farms in Munster and Leinster, Ireland. The company takes milk from their own farms to make award-winning artisan cheeses. The ethos of the company is local, co-operative, organic and family-orientated.

The Little Milk Company redesigned their website in 2014. The redesign was based on a number of customer insights. The company sells cheeses to retailers and distributors, and most buyers like to look at a supplier's website, before doing business. As sales increased and their market expanded abroad, the team wanted a website that met the needs of their customers.

The team began by identifying websites that they really liked. They attended a Google Analytics course run by Google for small businesses. They spent time thinking about the needs of their customers. Finally, they selected Emagine, a website design company they felt could deliver the quality and image that they wanted for The Little Milk Company.

The Little Milk Company were aware that they had to explain who they were, up front. So the top banner of the website's homepage simply describes The Little Milk Company, its cheeses and details about where they can be sampled and bought. According to the designers, Emagine, on 'the previous website, the story of the food was lost. It didn't demonstrate what makes The Little Milk Company unique. Information on available cheeses was nowhere in sight, the farmers and cheesemakers weren't represented at all. We implemented clear calls to action and removed any ambiguity. And we placed their products at centre stage.'

The striking aspect of the website is the imagery. The cheeses are artfully presented and there are wonderfully natural portraits of the farmers themselves.

In 2015, thelittlemilkcompany.ie won an award for the most beautiful website in Ireland.

What can we learn from a website like this that is beautiful and sticky and delivers incisive, customer-focused information? Here are three key points:

1. Imagery

The Little Milk Company uses high quality photography to illustrate their brand and it works brilliantly. The old saying that 'a picture tells a thousand words' is especially true for websites. Spare the words and use high quality images to engage customers. (Check out noho.ie for expertise in use of stunning digital imagery.) Your images should support your brand or the unique identity of your company.

2. Customer value

Your website has to immediately meet the needs and desires of the customer. The Little Milk Company achieves this by providing the most valuable information up front, because they know what their target audience needs: information about their range of cheeses, its provenance (farms and farmers) and where to buy the cheeses. They then follow up with more detailed information. The lesson is to understand customers using insights and prioritise your website content so that customers can find what they need easily.

3. Personality

The Little Milk Company show how a website can be used to create a genuine personality for a business. While most websites will be neither radical nor ingenious, it is still important to convey a creative and energetic personality for your business online. Too many businesses are pedestrian. Do you want your business website to be pedestrian?

The Little Milk Company has a brilliantly designed website, produced by a small, artisan business with a focus on exactly who their customers are. What can you do to produce and maintain an excellent website? Your website should be a shop window to the world.

FIGURE 3.2 — SEVEN LESSONS LEARNED FROM
WEBSITES THAT DO IT WELL

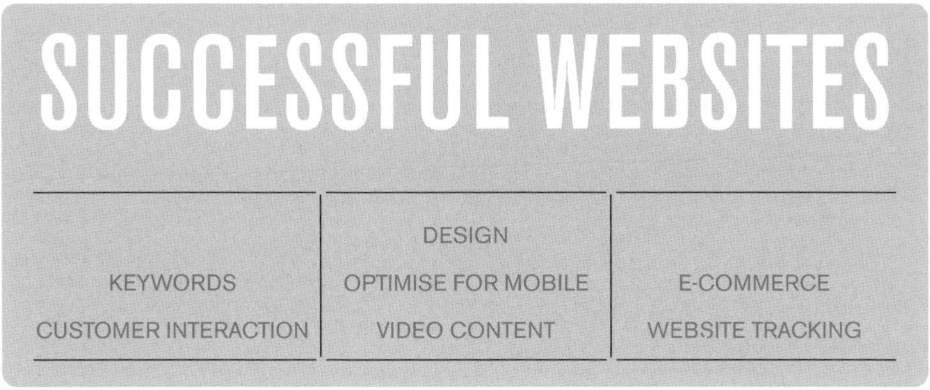

SUCCESSFUL WEBSITES

	DESIGN	
KEYWORDS	OPTIMISE FOR MOBILE	E-COMMERCE
CUSTOMER INTERACTION	VIDEO CONTENT	WEBSITE TRACKING

Seven lessons learned from websites that do it well

Keywords

How do people find websites online? The majority of people use search engines: Google, Yahoo and so on. They type in a keyword or a key phrase. What is a keyword? It's a high-performing word or phrase that people use to search for a product, service or solution through search engines or social media sites. Search engines trawl through the Internet using highly sophisticated algorithms or 'crawlers' to identify the websites they 'believe' most closely match the searcher's requirements.

Why are keywords important for your website? If your website does not have the keywords and phrases that a prospective customer uses to find a business of your type, then the search engines will never find you. For example, if you use the keyword phrase 'isotonic drink' and your customer searches for 'something to give me energy'. Insights are critical here. Talk to customers, listen to the language they use, then incorporate that keyword language throughout your site: homepage headings, body text and image descriptions, and test your keywords regularly, e.g. with Google's Keyword Tool. A well worked-out keyword strategy will be core to the success of your website.

Customer interaction

The priority of your website has to be meeting the needs of your customers by drawing on your knowledge of your target customers (see **Chapter 1**) and your ability to create impactful content (see **Chapter 2**).

Successful websites make every use of opportunities to interact with their customers, new and existing, and capture (more) information about them. **Figure 3.3** shows seven ways in which you can capture new customer leads and information for your business. These can be built into the structure of the homepage and also the key landing pages of the website. The Little Milk Company, for example, put a lot of thought into customer interaction on their homepage and throughout their site.

What's the difference between a homepage and a landing page?

Though the homepage is usually the front page of a website (its 'front door'), it is not always the first page that a person is directed to from a search engine. A landing page is a single web page that appears in response to clicking on a search-engine-optimised search result or an online advertisement. The customer could, and often does, bypass the homepage of the website and go directly to the page with the information that they want (e.g. the opening hours of the business) which is why it is important to also include customer interaction opportunities with landing pages.

JOIN OUR MAILING LIST

Encourage and entice
people to join your
emailing list in ways
that makes sense to
them (see **Chapter 6**)

CONTACT ME

It is becoming standard
to include a 'Contact me'
button on websites so
customers can register
their interest immediately

CONTACT NUMBER

Your contact number
should be on every
page and readily visible
at the top

EMAIL ADDRESS

An email address that is
checked regularly should
also be on every page

EVENTS

Whatever you can do to
invite customers to
participate in your business
is useful. Events are very
good for this: host webinars
or seminars, conferences,
open days, pop-up shops or
markets or a launch event
at your premises

LIVE CHAT

An online chat facility, if
you have the resources to
support it, can be very
powerful. Answer customer
queries immediately and
gain valuable, direct
insight into what customers
are looking for

MORE INFORMATION

What further information
interests your customer?
In return for their email
address, provide eBooks,
information sheets and
white papers, even pod-
casts and videos, about
topics of interest to your
customers. Use such interactions as an opportunity to
take leads to the next level

FIGURE 3.3 — SEVEN WAYS TO CAPTURE CUSTOMERS
FROM YOUR WEBSITE

Design

While most people would not be able to define good design, most of us know it when we see it. Most SMEs buy an 'off the shelf', low-cost website and adapt it to their needs. This is clearly cheaper than 'reinventing the wheel'. They often pay for the services of web designers to help them do this. Before committing any money, check out their previous work for other businesses to ensure they can do the work that will meet your customers's needs, including online ordering or booking facilities. Here are some guidelines to help you design or commission a wonderful website:

KEEP IT SIMPLE As you add new content, your website can become cluttered. Refresh and regenerate your website regularly to maintain clarity and ease of access. Make it simple, accessible and beautiful. Prioritise the information that customers will need and present those elements simply and effectively.

IMAGERY Aim to be creative, and original, where possible. If the option to commission bespoke images is beyond your budget, spend time creatively choosing stock images that reflect your business.

HARNESS YOUR BRAND When you set up your business, you probably commissioned a logo and brand image. Carry this branding look throughout your website and make sure it's in harmony with all the other elements that represent your brand – brochures, business cards, shop/office fronts and advertising.

RICH MEDIA Johos.at describes the journey of a coffee bean with fantastic story-telling, video, sound engineering and imagery. Find ways to entrance people who arrive on your website using the latest rich media technology.

SPEED OF LOADING One way to ensure a big 'bounce rate' is to have a 'heavy' slow-loading website. (Test the speed of your website at Pingdom.com.) If your pages take more than three seconds to load, there is a high risk that the people you have worked so hard to entice to your site will not hang around.

Optimise for mobile

Many, if not most, of your customers will have and regularly use smartphones, some of them exclusively, for going online. Is your website optimised and available to view on mobile devices? 90% of Irish people now have a smartphone (according to an Ipsos MORI Global Mobile Consumer Survey 2017, conducted on behalf of Deloitte). 71% have access to a tablet. Yet, the dot ie Digital Health Index report says that only 40% of company websites are adapted for mobile devices. What a missed opportunity. When redesigning your website, adopt a 'mobile first' approach, ensuring that it will work first and foremost on various mobile devices and can be enhanced further for access from PCs, etc. This way you can be sure that your customers are getting the best user experience, regardless of the device they are using.

Test how your website loads and appears on as many types of devices as you can. You cannot afford to lose this key segment of your audience because of poor performance on a mobile device.

Using the examples of online clothing retailer Boohoo and airline Ryanair, **Figure** 3.4 (over the page) outlines two different approaches to mobile-optimising websites, the first being to replicate the content of the 'main' site, the other adapting a more succinct version. **Figure** 3.5 then lists four key steps you can take towards the customer's mobile experience of your website being at least equal to if not better than that of the 'main' site.

Some legal considerations

Under data protection legislation, if you use cookies or collect personal data, such as email addresses, you must have a privacy statement on your website, setting out how your business complies with the data protection regulations. The ePrivacy Regulations state that consumers must consent to cookies before they can be used by your website. The e-Commerce Regulations set out the minimum information to be provided on a website. This information includes name, address, email address and VAT number of the service provider displayed in an accessible way.

FIGURE 3.4 — APPROACHES TO OPTIMISING WEBSITES FOR MOBILE

Develop your current website so that it can be seen and read easily on all digital platforms. Boohoo.com publishes the same content for desktops, laptops and mobile devices, from larger tablets to smaller smartphone screens.

APPROACHES TO OPTIMISING WEBSITES FOR MOBILE

Develop a specific, streamlined site for mobile, with less detail. When accessed from a mobile device, Ryanair.com has a more succinct menu and is dedicated to meeting key practical needs, e.g. booking and checking in.

FIGURE 3.5 — FOUR STEPS TO TAKE TO ACHIEVE MOBILE OPTIMISATION

CHECK YOUR WEBSITE ON VARIOUS DEVICES: TABLET, SMARTPHONE, DESKTOP/LAPTOP. DON'T FORGET TO CHECK DIFFERENCES BETWEEN MAKES AND OPERATING SYSTEMS.

PRIORITISE THE PARTS OF YOUR WEBSITE THAT ARE MOST IMPORTANT TO YOUR CUSTOMERS – FOR AIRLINES THESE INVOLVE BOOKING NEW FLIGHTS AND MANAGING EXISTING BOOKINGS. WHAT WILL YOUR CUSTOMER WANT TO DO AS A PRIORITY ON THE GO?

FOUR STEPS TO TAKE TO ACHIEVE MOBILE OPTIMISATION

TALK TO YOUR WEBSITE DEVELOPER ABOUT THE BEST OPTION FOR YOUR BUSINESS. SHOULD YOU ADAPT YOUR EXISTING SITE DESIGN OR SET UP A NEW MOBILE-OPTIMISED SITE? YOUR WEBSITE DEVELOPER WILL COST THESE OPTIONS OUT FOR YOU AND HELP YOU MAKE THE RIGHT DECISION.

PUT IN PLACE AN IMPLEMENTATION PLAN. DESIGNING, DEVELOPING, TESTING AND PAYING FOR THE NEW SITE ARE ALL ASPECTS THAT YOU NEED TO CONSIDER. USE THIS BOOK TO HELP YOU IDENTIFY ANY OTHER AMENDMENTS THAT YOU NEED TO MAKE TO YOUR WEBSITE AND PUT A DEVELOPMENT PLAN IN PLACE.

Video content
No one has time to read reams of information on a website. Video is one of the most powerful ways to tell people about your business, talk about your professional expertise, profile your involvement in the local community, etc. Make sure your videos are relevant to customer needs and motivations, and that they are short and concise. Take a look at webdoctor.ie for an example of a good home-page video.

"People turn to YouTube and they want to research, buy or fix a product…mobile watch time for apparel videos has doubled this year and videos about toys have also doubled. Google believes so strongly in the power of video that they recently added shopping ads to YouTube that allow people to make purchases directly within the video."

GOOGLE CEO SUNDAR PICHAL STATED DURING ALPHABET'S FIRST QUARTER EARNINGS CALL ON 22ND OCTOBER 2015 SOURCE: WIRED.COM (2015)

E-commerce
I mentioned that industry sectors tend to have specific off-the-shelf website packages available. These incorporate limited design and branding options with online booking, sales or reservation features. For example, many beauty and hair salons use the 'Phorest' software, which allows clients to book slots online and the salon to market new treatments, products and services to clients as they book.

Check out the reviews of the various packages available for your sector and speak to people who have already implemented the software to make sure that it meets your needs and the needs of your customers.

Website tracking
When you are setting up a website, make sure to put a web analytics package in place and constantly track the performance of your website. Tracking gives you insights into the behaviour of your online customers. It will also help you to focus and drive your content, design and product/service priorities in the future.

The most widely used tracking tool is Google Analytics which gives you website statistics to show you what is actually happening in your website. Google Analytics offers a range of useful options for e-commerce websites, including:

E-COMMERCE TRACKING Tracks your revenue and shows you how your customers found your store. Among other functions, it also helps you see which advertising mechanisms provide the best return.

GOAL TRACKING AND FUNNEL VISUALISATION Helps you to optimise your checkout process so that a higher proportion of the visitors to your site make a purchase.

DASHBOARDS Provide an overview of your most vital statistics in one place.

Facebook offers a service called Facebook Pixels, which are codes that you can embed in your website to track behaviour resulting from Facebook advertisements, such as browsing and purchasing (see **Chapter 5**).

BONUS – 10 WINNING WEBSITE CUSTOMER CALLS TO ACTION

1. CUSTOMER NEWSLETTERS
Make the content relevant, well designed and limit the quantity of newsletters that you send. Include 'buy now' offers, and unique deals for subscribers only. A great example of a subscriber newsletter is one offered by the Salthouse Inn, a hotel in Cape Cod (Salthouseinn.com – "get on the Salt House list and be in the know").

2. IMAGERY
Most people prefer to look at visuals – pictures and videos – rather than reading or listening. Nobo.ie, Wordbird.ie and Thelittlemilkcompany.ie are excellent for powerful imagery.

3. CALL-BACK REQUEST
Sometimes all people want is to speak to someone. Health clinics are particularly good at giving people the opportunity to request a call-back. The key is to 'wow' the customer by doing it in less than five minutes.

4. CONTACT US BUTTON

Add a 'Contact Us', button to every page and enable people to submit a contact request form with minimal effort. See the 123.ie Contact Us page at 123.ie/about-us/contact-us and how they qualify the nature of each lead with a simple drop-down menu directing queries to the right area.

5. LIVE CHAT

Though Live Chat takes resources and may not always be practical for a smaller business, I recently came across a small, online work-uniform company called Happythreads.ie, which offers a live chat facility operated by a receptionist who also handles in-bound phone calls.

6. FOLLOW US ON SOCIAL MEDIA

You are probably familiar with the symbols that indicate that a business has Facebook, Twitter, Pinterest and Instagram profiles. Use these symbols and links to encourage people who land on your website to follow your business on social media.

7. FREE TRIAL

Netflix has used the free-trial method of attracting customers with very good success. Many software companies have to offer a free trial to attract new sales. Just make sure there is a time limit and the ability to get in touch with those on the free trial to encourage sign up for the paid-for option.

8. SPECIAL INTRODUCTORY OFFER

Use special offers to continually stimulate and encourage lapsed customers to reengage with your services. Photobox.com continually offers special introductory offers and, if you have not used their services for a while, they send a new introductory offer or a money-off voucher to encourage you to try the service again.

9. REQUEST A CALL OUT / QUOTE

Tradesmen.ie provides a list of registered and experienced tradesmen. If a person needs a particular service, they log a request and a registered tradesman gets in touch – all done online.

10. FOLLOW OUR BLOG

People like Seth Godin, the veteran marketing guru, write excellent blog posts that can be read on their website. Subscribing to the blog keeps Seth's followers up to date with his wisdom, insights and books.

AT A GLANCE   CHAPTER THREE

Your website is your shop window to the world. It reflects your brand, your business and the interest that you have in your customers. A website will generate customer leads if its designed well, has relevant content and useful and interactive contact information. So write your website from your customer's perspective.

While 80% of Irish businesses have a website, most have only a relatively static, 'postcard', version. Only 30% of Irish businesses can actually sell online and many customers today may find that frustrating. Certainly, of the €9 billion that Irish consumers spend online, most of it is going abroad. I'm sure you, like me, want to see that change and would prefer to keep that spend within the Irish market.

Remember to integrate your marketing well, which means that you should at least keep your website up to date with what's happening in your business. At the same time, keep what's happening within your business up to date with what's happening online.

Make sure that your website is mobile optimised. At the minimum, check the site on your smartphone and tablet and ensure that it works on those media. Or, you may want to adopt the mobile-first philosophy.

Different approaches can be taken to mobile-optimising websites, from replicating the content of the 'main' site to adapting/developing a more succinct, bespoke version.

CHAPTER FOUR
SOCIAL MEDIA

4

"Treat social media more like a telephone than a megaphone." SIMON TAM, HUFFINGTON POST

Create your own trusted network

Social media is about connecting people online and creating trusted networks of like-minded individuals – followers who share similar interests, thoughts, ideas and information. 71% of Irish smartphone users use them to access social media accounts (Irish Life – iReach Survey, March 2017).

Lon Safko, author of *The Social Media Bible: Tactics, Tools and Strategies for Business Success* (2012), says that social media promotes a two-way conversation between businesses and consumers, not the one-way pontification preferred by companies in the past. "People want education, news, product reviews, shared experience good and bad with people who they trust. Corporate messages are not trusted. The new way to sell is not to sell at all."

Social media should be a listening tool for businesses, rather than a broadcast tool. It is not the number of followers that determine your success on social media, rather the level of engagement with those followers and how much they are prepared to interact with you. Tracking that success is crucial and according to the dot ie Digital Health Index Q4 2017, 17% of small businesses use the analytics available to them.

How can social media work for your business?

How social media works for your business depends very much on what you want to achieve. Social media works if you want to:

TARGET YOUR AUDIENCE. 90% of Irish people use social media (according to the Mediacom Social Nation Report 2017). Just ask your customers. Most of them use social media in some form. Social media sites like Facebook, Instagram, LinkedIn and Twitter enable you to build a group of followers that you can stay in touch with.

NEW CUSTOMER ACQUISITION In **Chapter 1**, we talked a lot about market segments. Social media sites have the ability to target consumers to a high degree through their advertising platforms. You can choose by age profile, gender, interests, location, occupation, and a host of other elements, to target your preferred customer segments and personas. The forensic nature of social media marketing makes it cost-effective, if used properly. This allows you to hone your market from the start.

PROMOTE YOUR BRAND Search engines like social media. I mentioned search engine results pages (SERPS) in **Chapter 2**; if you want to achieve high rankings on SERPs, then social media can really help. Search engines want content to be fresh and relevant; social media activity, linking to your website will help ensure this. If you keep your social media channels up to date and relevant to your audience, and if the interaction with your posts is good (they are liked and shared), then search engines will take that into account when compiling their SERPs.

CONNECT WITH LIKE-MINDED PEOPLE Like-minded people tend to form groups and social media helps to globalise those groups. When The Gathering Ireland events were being set up in 2013, Facebook and Twitter were powerful tools in connecting with Irish people all over the world.

GET CUSTOMER INSIGHTS You can use social media to get an in-depth understanding of your customers from their social media interaction with you and your business, what they engage with, post and like.

Here is a story of a small Swiss village that achieved global attention, using Facebook:

CASE STUDY OBERMUTTEN: A LITTLE VILLAGE GOES GLOBAL – There is a region in Switzerland called Graubünden where there are many tiny, undiscovered villages, including Obermutten, which has 79 inhabitants, one hotel and one church.

In 2011, the Mayor of Obermutten decided to promote the town and engaged advertising agency Jung von Matt to run a digital marketing campaign on Facebook. The campaign invited people to 'Like' Obermutten's page and promised that everyone who did so would have their Facebook page printed out and stuck on to a bulletin board located in the centre of the village.

The campaign was so popular that within days the village bulletin board was full of Facebook pages. More bulletin boards were set up; as these overflowed, Facebook pages were put onto the sides of barns. Every villager got involved in an effort to deliver on the mayor's promise to print out every Facebook fan's page.

Within four weeks, Obermutten had fans in 32 countries and had become a world news sensation. A village of 79 people had over 12,000 Facebook fans – more fans than Florence or Helsinki. Four out of five fans are continuously interactive with the page, which is more than the Facebook pages of Lady Gaga, Coca-Cola and even Justin Bieber.

Sixty million people have read, seen or heard about Obermutten. The mayor of the village turned an investment of 10,000 Swiss francs in a Facebook marketing campaign into the media equivalent of a 2.4 million Swiss franc spend. Thousands of fans have promised to visit the town and hundreds already have.

Source: www.stateofdigital.com Facebook engagement – A Little Town called Obermutten.

The mayor and people of Obermutten have shown the power of social media to reach people all over the world. You just need a good angle and determination to succeed. While there are a number of things that we can learn from Obermutten, the most inspiring are shown in **Figure 4.1**:

FIGURE 4.1 — THREE LESSONS FROM OBERMUTTEN'S
FACEBOOK CAMPAIGN

SUPPORT FROM THE TOP	PROVIDE INSPIRATIONAL CONTENT	PAID ADVERTISING WORKS
SOCIAL MEDIA WORKS BEST WHEN TOP MANAGEMENT ARE INVOLVED. IT SHOULD BE A WHOLE COMPANY PROJECT.	PEOPLE LIKE INSPIRATIONAL, ENTERTAINING AND EDUCATIONAL CONTENT. YOUR SOCIAL MEDIA POSTS SHOULD REFLECT AT LEAST ONE OF THESE.	IN TODAY'S COMPETITIVE WORLD, IT PAYS TO LAUNCH YOUR SOCIAL MEDIA PROFILES BY BUYING ONLINE ADVERTISING TO AMPLIFY YOUR MESSAGE.

Social media is a great customer service tool

Social media is now widely used for managing customer service. Many companies no longer answer frequently asked questions (FAQs) on their websites. Instead, they answer customer queries on Twitter, Facebook or by using a live chat facility (see **Chapter 3**). Customer questions can be answered in real time and is easier to get an overview of and monitor queries and concerns. For example, airlines typically use Twitter to keep passengers up-to-date on flight delay status.

Social media promotes your brand

Effective use of your social media channels, buttons and links for which you can put on your website, business cards, advertisements and marketing material, will contribute to the search-engine ranking of your website thereby promoting it and your brand.

According to the dot ie Digital Health Index (see **Figure 4.2**), the social media channels that Irish businesses favour are: Facebook, LinkedIn, Twitter and YouTube. Instagram is also rapidly gaining popularity for business marketing. Let's examine how you can maximise these for your business, in more detail.

Social media working for your business

Figure 4.3 opposite synopsises a selection of the most popular social media channels used by businesses. The statistics and metrics, including the global MAU (monthly active users) change frequently, and are correct as of January 2017. This chart compares the various social media sites and is intended to help you consider what your social media assets can do for your business.

FIGURE 4.2 — WHAT DIGITAL ASSETS DO IRISH SMEs CURRENTLY HAVE?
(SOURCE: DOT IE DIGITAL HEALTH INDEX — Q4 2017)

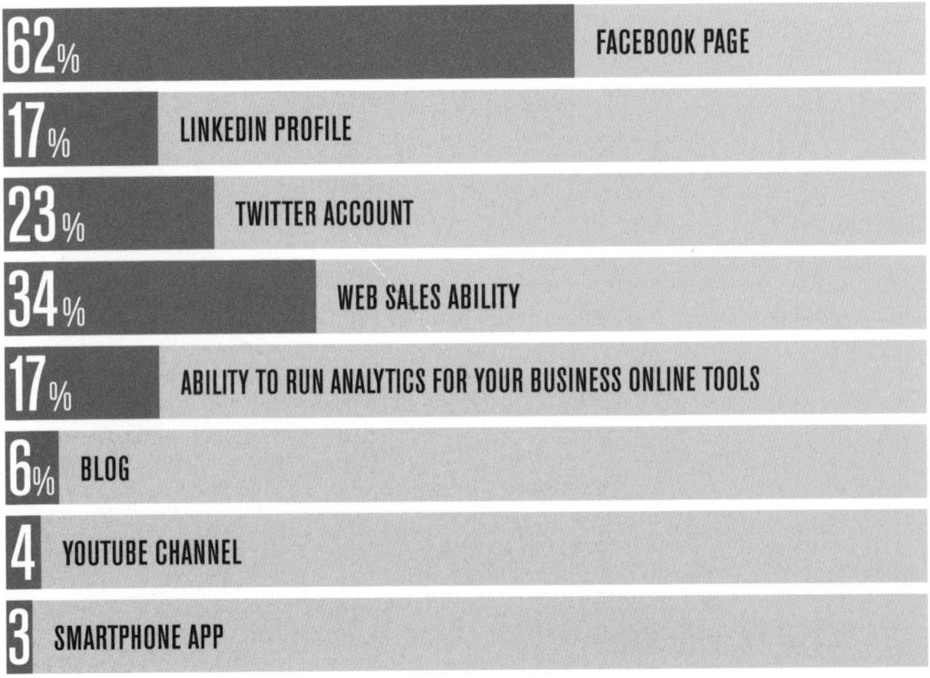

62% FACEBOOK PAGE

17% LINKEDIN PROFILE

23% TWITTER ACCOUNT

34% WEB SALES ABILITY

17% ABILITY TO RUN ANALYTICS FOR YOUR BUSINESS ONLINE TOOLS

6% BLOG

4 YOUTUBE CHANNEL

3 SMARTPHONE APP

FIGURE 4.3 — WHAT SOCIAL MEDIA SITES CAN DO FOR YOUR BUSINESS
(SOURCES: DOT IE DIGITAL HEALTH INDEX Q4 2017, STATISTA.COM, IPSOS SOCIAL
NETWORKING TRACKER 2017, STATISTA.COM (JANUARY 2017)

SOCIAL MEDIA SITE	WHAT IT DOES FOR BUSINESS
Facebook Facebook is where people connect with friends and family.	2,070 million monthly active users (MAU). Facebook is the most popular social media platform in Ireland. 64% of all Irish adults use Facebook. Over 70% of Irish businesses have a Facebook page. **Pages** Facebook for business is called a 'Page' and is easy to set up. Facebook provides a timeline for your business: consumers can see the progress and the interactions on your page, in chronological order. Facebook Pages for business give you the option to target age groups, locations and gender – and a number of other criteria – for marketing campaigns.
Twitter Twitter is where people find out what's happening in the world right now.	330 million MAU and over 500 million tweets per day. (Source: Twitter Inc.) 2% of Irish businesses have a Twitter account or profile. 28% of Irish people have a Twitter account. **Engagement** 50% of Twitter users have visited or shopped at the websites of the small businesses they follow on Twitter. **Customers** 40% of followers of business Twitter accounts plan to purchase regularly from the small businesses they follow. Good customer service tool – the business can quickly respond to service queries. **Sales** 60% of Twitter users purchased from a small business because of something they saw on Twitter. **Research** The business can keep up with its industry, competition and customers.
Instagram A mobile photo-sharing, video-sharing, and social networking application.	27% of Irish adults use Instagram, which is owned by Facebook. 800 million MAU makes it the second largest social media site after Facebook and it is growing rapidly. 95 million+ photos shared per day. Businesses can promote their brand by using images and short videos – there are now one million advertisers on Instagram up from 200,000 in 2016. Tells the story of your business with images. Allows you to embed an image or video into your blog.

FIGURE 4.3 CONT. — WHAT SOCIAL MEDIA SITES CAN DO FOR YOUR BUSINESS
(SOURCES: DOT IE DIGITAL HEALTH INDEX Q4 2017, STATISTA.COM, IPSOS SOCIAL
NETWORKING TRACKER 2017, STATISTA.COM (JANUARY 2017))

LinkedIn The world's largest professional online network.	More than 467 million members and over 100 million MAUs in over 200 countries and territories. A LinkedIn Company Page "helps others learn more about your business, brand, products and services, and job opportunities". Approximately 17% of Irish businesses have a LinkedIn Company Page. 27% of Irish adults have a LinkedIn profile.
YouTube YouTube allows billions of people to discover, watch and share videos online.	YouTube is the second largest search engine in the world, after Google. Globally, YouTube has over 1.3 billion MAU. Approximately 4% of Irish SMEs have a YouTube channel.

FIGURE 4.4 — HOW TO MAKE SOCIAL MEDIA WORK
FOR YOUR BUSINESS

CREATE YOUR
PAGE

HOW TO MAKE SOCIAL MEDIA

BUILD YOUR
COMMUNITY

Create your business page or profile

Each of the social media sites outlined in the preceding pages enable businesses to set up 'Pages' or 'Profiles' and you can use these to help you promote your business and, more importantly, to interact with consumers.

Additionally, the main social media platforms have page-management systems that enable you to see how many people like or follow your page, how many clicked on or shared your posts or tweets or photo images. This reporting functionality helps you to hone your posts so that you can constantly improve in meeting the motivations of potential customers.

What sort of posts should you put up on your business pages?

To partly recall the quote from Lon Safko at the beginning of this chapter, "Corporate messages are not trusted. The new way to sell is not to sell at all." Customers have been turned off and they have revolted – blocking businesses that bombard them with marketing messages that they judge to be irrelevant to them and their lives.

When it comes to tweets, Facebook posts, LinkedIn posts and other social media posts, I advocate a 80/20 rule that will keep your balance correct, for consumers:

- 80% of your content should simply provide useful information relevant to your customer, but linking in some way to the overall business. People will trust you more if you are not selling all the time.
- 20% of your social media content can then be directly about your business, products or services for promotion purposes, 'such as posts and tweets about new products or features, launches, sales pitches, special offers, and so forth.

All of this social media activity generates fresh content and keeps your social media channels dynamic. In linking back to your website, building your social media activity and community will contribute to its popularity and drive consumer traffic.

TWO-WAY FLOW OF COMMUNICATION

RUN YOUR CAMPAIGNS

WORK FOR YOUR BUSINESS

TRACK YOUR SUCCESS

Build your community

Once you have created your Page, you will want to build a community of followers. When a person follows your social media pages or channels, they are open to receiving more information about your business and brands. They may also interact, posting comments, images and stories of their own.

Quality vs quantity

How important are 'Likes' and 'Followers' on social media? Some commentators argue that the main aim should be to build the largest possible community of likes, others that it is the *quality* of the likes and their on-going interaction with your Facebook page that is important.

Robert Kelly of Kong Digital emphasises that you have to target the *right* people: "96% of people who like a Facebook page never actually return to that page", he says. "However, if you do it right, they will. Target the right people to get the right likes. If your posts get a lot of interaction, comments, likes and are posted onwards, then they will in turn stay on timelines longer."

Two-way flow of communication

Real-time, interactive communication with customers is a real benefit of using social media. (Íarnrod Éireann (@IrishRail) manage customer updates very effectively on Twitter.) If you are running your own, smaller business, you don't have to be in the office to deal with customer queries and concerns – social media enables you to respond to their questions on the go.

Crowd-sourced content

As we saw in **Chapter 2**, if content is king, user-generated content is emperor. The enormous benefit of online digital media is its ability to get people interacting, sharing, commenting, comparing and story-telling. Whenever you can, open up the opportunity for customers, prospective customers, employees and others who might have an interest in your business to contribute to your social media pages. Encourage members of your online community to post content with story-telling, events, news, photos, testimonials, new ideas and competitions.

Run your campaign

Social media enables you to attract new customers using promotional discounts, vouchers and deals. It also allows you to engage in dialogue with followers and capture their feedback, both positive and negative. Above all, social media gives you a captive audience: people who openly declare that they are interested in your business. Today, you can launch a social media campaign and follow it up with advertising that directly targets those who have responded. If you use it the right way, social media can be extremely targeted and effective without being cost indulgent.

Your customers and prospective customers can follow your progress and scroll back through it to see new initiatives, launches and stories. Only social media and, in particular, Facebook, Instagram and Twitter, allow you to display your company/ brand history in this way. This means that customers and prospective customers can get an image-laden overview of your business, which gives them an understanding of its values and ethos of. Look up The Little Milk Company on Facebook for an excellent timeline profile of a business on social media.

Social media sites use algorithms to evaluate business pages and to highlight those companies that most closely satisfy a person's requirements, when they are searching using keywords. The algorithm places a weighting on the type of posts that a business uses:

- Images and video content have the strongest weighting.
- If you include a link to a website or a shared link, then that gets a strong weighting.
- Worded content such as articles and PDFs without images are rated as least important.

This means that each of your social media campaign posts should be accompanied by image and/or video where possible.

In **Chapter 1**, I mentioned that emotional triggers help to attract customers. If you can elicit a positive emotional response towards your brand, this will help attract more customers online. Your digital marketing campaigns should reflect real emotion, authenticity and passion. Use stories, for example, to trigger an emotional response from your followers, one that engenders greater interest and loyalty. Try to engender a spirit of communion in a world in which personal isolation is one of the greatest problems.

Finally, be true to yourself. There's no point creating an image of an organisation that is not truly reflected in your brand, your people or your other promotional material. All your work should be interconnected and present a real face to followers, friends and customers – otherwise you will soon be found out and 'Unliked'.

Track success

Social-media tracking and performance measurement makes social networks very user-friendly for business. All of the social media platforms have analytics services attached to them. Here is a brief summary of just some of the capability:

FACEBOOK PAGE INSIGHTS shows you which posts customer engage with and which they have less interest in. That means that you can track your successes and build on them to improve the performance of your posts.

TWITTER ANALYTICS enables you to monitor and improve your tweeting performance. This functionality enables you to measure your followers' engagement and shows you how to improve your performance. You can also analyse the demographics, interests and locations of your followers.

LINKEDIN ANALYTICS gives businesses information about their company pages. You can get updates on your followers, visitors to your LinkedIn pages and the performance of company updates. Analytics shows you the level of engagement of your posts, as well as giving you insights into trends, demographics and page traffic.

YOUTUBE INSIGHTS provides analytics on every video posted. It can give you statistics on uploaded videos that were viewed, as well as demographics information. Interestingly, YouTube also provides information on how videos are discovered online.

A word about social media for professionals

There is some debate among professionals as to the use of social media in promoting them and their services. In my opinion, social media can really work for professionals. Which social media you use depends on the type of professional service you offer. LinkedIn is essential for providing clear information and details about professional firms, their representative employees and is excellent for B2B marketing.

Twitter enables professionals to comment on topics of the day and it is a great way to interact with the media and with other commentators. It also works for professionals who want to communicate with potential clients.

More and more professionals are using Facebook to profile their services, team members and to interact with clients. As we have seen, Facebook gives you the facility to profile your firm using imagery, video and blog-type articles. It fosters affinity and helps you to build a community of followers, which keeps you in front of your client-base, prospective clients and influencers. Facebook allows you to develop your brand and communicate aspects of your service that you might normally not get to highlight with less interactive media.

Instagram and YouTube can also be useful to professionals. Instagram works brilliantly for designers and architects and others who communicate visually. YouTube works for all organisations, though the video quality has to be of an excellent standard – or it can detract from your brand.

Figure 4.5 below provides a brief analysis, in a B2B context, of how professional services firms can and do use social media to showcase what they do and the kind of content they can post:

FIGURE 4.5 — TYPICAL PROFESSIONAL SERVICES FIRMS SOCIAL MEDIA POSTS

PROFESSIONAL FIRMS

AWARDS WON

ARTICLES ON CURRENT/ RELEVANT TOPICS

BLOG POSTS

CAREER OPPORTUNITIES

DATES TO REMEMBER

ECONOMIC UPDATES

EVENT PHOTO GALLERIES

INDUSTRY OUTLOOKS

MEET THE TEAM/SENIOR PARTNERS

PODCASTS ON TOPICAL AREAS

POSING FUNDAMENTAL QUESTIONS, E.G. 'HAS YOUR ORGANISATION A FORMAL RISK APPETITE STATEMENT?'

TECHNICAL ARTICLES

PR ARTICLES

SENIOR PARTNER INTERVIEWS

STRATEGIC REPORTS

SURVEYS

WEBINARS

WHITE PAPERS

AT A GLANCE   CHAPTER FOUR

At first, social media was purely social – a way to connect with school friends, colleagues and even old flames. Now social media is available for and used extensively by business. You can set up pages for your business and interact with those who 'Like' or 'Follow' it.

Social media pages are excellent for generating customer leads. Your page or profile followers become willing recipients for your stories, promotions and brand attributes because they have chosen to 'Like' or 'Follow' you. Very often, they are willing to share positive stories about their interaction with your business and such loyal contributors to your social media pages are wonderfully valuable.

Businesses can use social media for so many things – to communicate the brand and product or service updates, FAQs, to provide customer response services and, in times of emergency, to keep customers informed of progress (e.g. power lines down during storms), and much more.

There are a number of rules to follow to ensure that your social media pages and profiles continue to be liked. Don't make them all about sales and marketing – include educational, entertaining and inspirational content.

Use a variety of media including imagery, catchy headlines and video. In doing so, harness the look and feel of your brand. Always try to brand your social media pages so that your company can be easily identified and recognised.

CHAPTER FIVE
ONLINE ADVERTISING

An early caveat: online advertising is complex, resource-indulgent (one often needs deep pockets) and good returns can be elusive unless you are really sure of what you want to achieve. For truly effective campaigns, it is wise to seek advice from experts experienced in using the various advertising platforms and the frenetic pace of adaptation required.

Paid amplification

Up to now we have discussed your ideal customer, development and branding of your website and social media channels, as well as the kinds of interactive, sticky content you will need. How in this world of millions upon millions of websites and social media pages do you ensure your audience visits yours? Could advertising be the answer?

The next digital marketing technique that you may wish to consider is online advertising. Online advertising is often referred to as 'paid amplification', meaning that you pay to get your message to the target segments you wish to attract to your digital media assets. In a report for the Irish government in 2016, Indecon International Economic Consultants stated that:

"Online advertising is now the fastest growing form of business advertising in Ireland, growing at over 20% in each of the last four years. It has become a much larger portion of total advertising expenditure, reaching over 20% of total spend in 2015, with broadcast and print advertising both seeing falling shares."

There are a wide range of online advertising options including mobile phone advertising which is now the most popular, as well as, advertising on SERPs, display adverts on websites, video advertising, and a whole host of social media advertising opportunities.

It is important to be tactical with online advertising, depending on the size of your business. Few small businesses have the cash to engage in advertising for the long-term.

It is impossible to ignore digital advertising today. It now significantly outstrips traditional advertising in terms of advertisement expenditure and the greatest growth is seen in mobile phone advertising where mobile adspend is higher than desktop PC adspend. Social media advertising and video advertising are also huge growth areas. Digital advertising is set to grow by up to 17% per annum up to 2020.

How does online advertising differ from traditional advertising?

With online advertising you can target your ideal customers directly. Online advertising platforms, such as Google's Adwords for example, help you to precisely identify the audience that you want your advertisement to reach. The online booking platforms allow you to choose gender, age, location, interests and even the behaviours of the market segments that you want to view your ads. In **Chapter 1**, we looked at market segment targeting and persona profiling. Many of the social media and search engine advertising platforms, particularly Facebook, Instagram and Twitter, allow you to plug this detail into your booking information, so that you can direct your advertising to the right market.

The second compelling aspect of online advertising is that its design capability spans a wide range of formats, styles and designs from text only, to imagery and text, to video. Online advertising can also include rich or interactive media – such as games, competitions, and all sorts of entertainment.

A third key advantage of online advertising is that, when clicked on, it will link potential customers directly through to your website, online store or social media pages. You can track the performance of an advertisement by measuring the click-throughs to your business pages, monitor the length of time that a person spends on your website and determine whether they actually made a purchase or not.

FIGURE 5.1 — ONLINE AD SPEND OF IRISH BUSINESSES IN 2016
(SOURCE: IAB / PWC ONLINE ADSPEND STUDY FOR THE YEAR ENDED DECEMBER 2016)

TYPE OF ONLINE ADVERTISING	BRIEF DESCRIPTION	% INCREASE IN SPEND 2015 v 2016
Paid-for-search represents a spend of €219 million or 49% of online advertising spend.	Search advertisements are the ads that appear on SERPs on both PCs and smart phones. When someone uses a keyword for which you have paid on a search engine and your ad appears then you pay each time the person searching actually clicks on your ad – known as pay per click (PPC). Paid-for-search also works for search engines on smartphones.	25%
Display advertising represents a spend of €197 million or 45% of total advertising spend.	Online display advertisements are banner adverts designed to entice people to click on them. By clicking, a consumer is typically linked back to a website of a business of specific product/service, or they can interact with the ad itself, e.g. as a game. Display ads are presented in many forms ranging from smaller 'buttons' of different dimensions, to columns reaching from top to bottom of a web page ('skyscrapers'), to full page ads. Display ads can be text-only, image-based, video or entertainment forms, such as interactive games. Native advertising is advertising that reflects or looks the same as the website it appears on. Often called 'sponsored' or 'promo-tioned content'.	44%
	The advertising charging model for online display ads can be PPC (see above) or cost per thousand (CPM), i.e. the price of 1,000 ad impressions on one webpage, or a combination of both models.	
	Display ads can appear on websites, SERPs, emails, social media pages and video channels.	
	In Ireland, from 2015 to 2016:	
	• Social media display advertising enjoyed significant growth.	133%
	• Mobile phone display advertising showed consistent growth.	63%
	• Digital video advertising grew by:	91%
	• Native advertising	82%
Classified advertising held its position at €29 million or 6% share of the total advertising spend.	Online classified ads appear on specialist sales websites such as Adverts.ie, Carzone.ie and DoneDeal.ie	2%

Online advertising in Ireland

IAB Ireland, in association with PwC, regularly carry out an online adspend study, to find out where and how much advertisers spend online in the Irish market and how. In 2016, the online advertising spend was €445 million, up by 31% on the previous year.

In **Chapter 3**, I emphasised the importance of anticipating searchers' keywords and key word phrases in the development of your website. Keywords are also very important in online advertising. If your advertisements can reflect the language the customer uses to find a product or a service, then your advertisements will have greater impact.

Online advertising goes viral

The fastest growing online advertising mechanism is video advertising. According to an IAB Ireland report carried out by Nielsen, "The Power of VOD 3" (June 2016): "Video advertising drives brand growth – 24% of adults visit a brand's website after seeing a video ad and 20% search online for the specific brand." There are so many brilliant video advertisements and they are not as expensive to create as you may think. Some use celebrities; for example, the Dublin Bus "Mad Dash Home" campaign sought to put a human face on the brand and educate the public about the people and technology at the control centre of the city's bus transport system, and did so successfully by featuring various Irish celebrities in their videos. Others are amusing, like the Voltarol dancing banner advert. Others use games to promote a message, such as the Men's Cancer Alliance Keepy Uppy game (see **Chapter 2**).

One of the most successful online advertisers is the Blendtec company. They chose a very simple digital video advertising campaign to market their blenders.

CASE STUDY   BLENDTEC — Blendtec is a small Utah-based business that makes superior quality food blenders. In 2006, the company found that people were not aware of Blendtec and their powerful blenders. The company had an impossibly small budget of $50 to launch an advertising campaign.

George Wright, the company's marketing director, decided to launch a cheap digital video advertising campaign called 'Will it Blend?'. George Wright purchased marbles, cans of Diet Coke, a McDonald's Happy Meal, a rotisserie chicken and a garden rake. He made videos of founder Tom Dickson, dressed in a white coat and protective glasses, blending these items.

Since 2006, Dickson has starred in more than 165 videos. iPads, lighters, pool cues, footballs, you name it, Tom Dickson has blended it. The campaign continues with Apple watches and a variety of other premium items queued for online blending.

In 2007, revenue at Blendtec increased by 500%. Blendtec still invites people to suggest what they want blended next on www.facebook.com/willitblend. To date, they have had more than 500 million views on YouTube and the campaign has won accolades all over the world.

Source: CNNmoney.com, "Pureé a Rake for Fun and Profit" (April 2008)

Surprise, emotion and engagement (SEE)

Keeping in mind the award-winning Blendtec campaign and the advice of David Meerman Scott in his book *The Book of Marketing and PR*, **Figure 5.2** below outlines what makes video ad campaigns successful.

FIGURE 5.2 — THREE KEY ELEMENTS OF VIDEO AD CAMPAIGNS
(SOURCE: DAVID MEERMAN SCOTT, THE NEW RULES OF MARKETING AND PR)

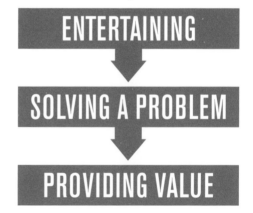

Entertaining

Tom Dickenson's claim that his Blendtec product can blend anything is not surprising. Watching him mash up the latest iPad in a blender, however, is entertaining and entertainment is Blendtec's greatest asset in its online advertising.

In the **Introduction**, I mentioned how consumers are bombarded with advertising and marketing messages online. Many prefer to have fun. Remember also, that Millennials, in particular, are the thrill-seeking generation. They're looking to be entertained. So target your video advertising towards people who have a FOMO (fear of missing out). No matter what advertising you develop, part of your advertising brief has to be to deliver an element of surprise – something unique, amusing, emotive or even a little shocking (in a positive way, of course).

Solving a problem

Your customer insights will prove very useful. Going online, what is the problem that your customers are trying to solve, the need they want to answer? Can you use your online advertising to solve that problem, meet that need? Whether you run a pay-for-search advertising campaign through Google Adwords, or you develop advertisements to display on online media or you develop your own video advertising campaign – think 'Problem Solving'. Again, focus on emotive content that will deeply engage the viewer, harnessing their motivations and issues.

Blendtec's problem-solving message answers anyone looking for a high quality, highly effective and durable food blender.

Providing value

Value is what you give to customers for the money you charge. In your advertising message, it is important to show the value that you provide to customers. So, in developing your online ads, provide something that a customer will see as valuable to them, such as a special offer, free sample, late opening hours, etc. If they see the value in you, they will become a valued customer to you.

From advertising concept to implementation

In planning to deliver your entertaining, problem-solving and value-driven advertising messages to your audience, consider which advertising platforms to use. There is a bewildering amount of choice available and you have to choose a small number of platforms that will appeal most to your potential customers. Design is important too. You have to stand out from the herd.

Figure 5.3 offers a selection of the more popular advertising options available to you, which are then discussed in turn.

FIGURE 5.3 — SEVEN TYPES OF ONLINE ADVERTISING

SEVEN TYPES OF ONLINE ADVERTISING

GOOGLE MY BUSINESS LISTING

PAID-FOR-SEARCH/ GOOGLE ADWORDS

DISPLAY AND NATIVE ADVERTISING

SOCIAL MEDIA ADVERTISING

MOBILE ADVERTISING

GEO-LOCATION ADVERTISING

BEHAVIOURAL ADVERTISING

Google My Business listing

Google My Business is a free business listing on Google Search and Google Maps. Every business should have this. It is free. See www.google.com/business for how you can get your business listed on the Google SERP. List your business hours, phone numbers and directions on Google Search and on Google Maps. Include images of your business to make it stand out. Once it is set up and verified by you, customers can find you online, locate you, post reviews and get the latest information about your business.

Paid-for-search/Google AdWords

Google AdWords is the largest online advertising platform in the world. Google AdWords allows you to easily produce and launch your own online advertisements. When you enter a keyword or phrase in Google, ads appear at the top, bottom or sides of the results page (SERP). Google AdWords is a type of search-engine marketing, which is different to SEO (see **Chapter 8**). Google charges using the pay-per-click (PPC) model, meaning Google charges a fee each time someone uses a keyword for which you have paid and your ad appears in the search results. Then, you pay each time the person searching actually clicks on your ad. This makes search-engine marketing very measurable.

Display and native advertising

Online display advertising can include:

- Text (or native content): just text to promote your business.
- Standard display: images and basic interactivity with no expansion.
- Rich media: highly interactive rich media incuding games, video and opportunities to interact with the ad.

Consumers today tend to engage less with banner ads; they are frequently seen as a nuisance and are sometimes even blocked. 'Native advertising' is sponsored content that sits within and resembles the editorial content of a website; it is more accepted by consumers. It isn't as intrusive and is more often seen as informative content than advertising. Native advertising has begun to overtake traditional online display and should be incorporated into your digital ad campaigns.

Display and native advertisements can be targeted towards your specific target audience. However, it is worthwhile getting some expert advice before you commit resources to designing advertisements and placing display ads. Both design and placement of advertisements require specialist knowledge. There are lots of agencies and freelance advisors who specialise in online marketing for small businesses. It is important to be clear about your target market segments, keywords and your budget when designing your online advertising campaign.

RICH MEDIA

- RICH MEDIA ALLOWS YOU OR YOUR AGENCY TO CREATE COMPLEX OR MORE EFFECTIVE ADVERTISEMENTS. IT USES FLASH OR HTML TECHNOLOGY AND CAN INCLUDE MULTIPLE LEVELS OF MEDIA INCLUDING VIDEO AND GAMES. RICH MEDIA EXCELS AT GENERATING BRAND AWARENESS AND FOR ATTRACTING ATTENTION.

- BLENDTEC'S 'WILL IT BLEND?' CAMPAIGN USES RICH MEDIA IN THE FORM OF VIDEO. THE SHELF LIFE OF BLENDTEC RICH MEDIA IS FAR LONGER THAN ANY TEXT OR DISPLAY ADVERTISEMENT, WHICH, UNLESS YOU SPEND MONEY DAILY, ONLY HAS A SHORT TIME-SPAN IN FRONT OF YOUR TARGET AUDIENCE.

- THE ARGUMENT FOR USING RICH MEDIA IS STRONG. RESEARCH FROM THE UNIVERSITY OF MINNESOTA SUGGESTS THAT PRESENTATIONS USING VISUAL AIDS ARE 43% MORE PERSUASIVE THAN UNAIDED PRESENTATIONS. 93% OF OUR COMMUNICATION IS NON-VERBAL. CONSUMERS LIKE VIDEO.

- FORRESTER RESEARCH ESTIMATES THAT RICH MEDIA GENERATED OVER 70% OF DIGITAL REVENUE IN 2016.

- FINALLY, A CAVEAT: WE MAY WANT TO GENERATE THE PERFECT, EXCITING GLOBAL, VIRAL ADVERTISING SENSATION, BUT THIS WILL BE ELUSIVE. FOR MOST OF US. RICH MEDIA IS COSTLY, COMPLEX AND DIFFICULT TO GET RIGHT. IT REQUIRES MORE RESOURCES, TECHNOLOGY AND TESTING THAN TEXT OR STANDARD ONLINE DISPLAY ADVERTISEMENTS.

Social media advertising

The last chapter looked at social media, how to set up pages, produce posts and attract 'Likes', digital marketing activity that is free. It is also possible to pay for advertising on social media pages and channels.

The major social media platforms – Facebook, Twitter, LinkedIn, Instagram and YouTube – all provide advertising platforms to help you promote your brand or product to a select target audience. The range of opportunities within each of these social media sites for advertising is very wide.

The various social media advertising platforms, similar in style to Google AdWords, allow you to be specific about the people you want to target.

Advertising is very popular and rated as successful on social media, because it can tap into consumers' interests and behaviours. Social media adverts that appear on a consumer's Facebook page are more likely to be clicked on, than general display advertisements, which tend to be less targeted.

So, which social media platforms or networks should you advertise on?

The top three channels are:

1. Facebook

2. Instagram

3. Twitter

Facebook advertising
You, as a business person, design an advertisement and decide who you want to see that advertisement. Facebook is particularly targeted. For example, if you want to sell jumpers to people aged 18–35 who go skiing each winter and like to spend on luxury goods, then you could use Facebook to this specific audience. Facebook then distributes the advertisement to the profiles that you have specified. The key to effective Facebook advertising is having a high click-through rate (CTR). Achieving a high CTR involves a combination of a powerful image, an engaging headline, and razor-sharp audience targeting.

Facebook also offers you the opportunity to promote posts that were particularly popular among the followers of your business. The useful thing about this method is that you get the chance to test your posts first and then promote the best ones.

I also mentioned in **Chapter 3** that you can include Facebook Pixels on your website to monitor the behaviour of people who respond to your Facebook advertising.

Instagram advertising
Instagram is the fastest growing social media platform and there are over 25 million businesses with profiles on Instagram. Instagram is owned by Facebook and uses the Facebook advertising platform. It allows you to advertise using photo, video, carousel and Instagram stories.

Twitter advertising
Similarly, with Twitter you can specify your audience for an advertisement in some detail. Twitter offers a range of advertising options including: website cards, follower campaigns, engagement campaigns and mobile app promotions.

Mobile advertising

More people buy smartphones than PCs. Consumers want to be able to transact on the go. As a result, Google and Facebook are moving more and more of their focus and investment to mobile advertising.

This is a relatively new medium and you are probably seeing more mobile advertising on your phone than before. It is now a critical channel for marketers.

Mobile advertising is a significant advertising tool for business. Mobile advertising represents 52% of digital advertising in Ireland. Consumers have a 'mobile first' mindset and this opens up the opportunity for mobile advertising. Mobile advertising is mainly divided between search advertising and display advertising, but also includes SMS texts and ads run within mobile apps (see **Figure 5**.4 below). You may wish to engage with a mobile display advertising partner. These companies help you to place mobile ads optimally so that your audience is neatly targeted.

M-commerce is mobile e-commerce and this is something that all small businesses can benefit from.

FIGURE 5.4 — TYPES OF MOBILE ADVERTISING

TYPES OF AD	DESCRIPTION
SMS text messages	Having received permission from the customer, text their mobile phone with special promotions, offers or updates. This is an ideal way to keep regular customers informed of special deals.
Mobile search ads	These ads are similar to paid-for-search ads, e.g. on Google AdWords, only with fewer ads on display. Mobile search ads show up on mobile search engines on SERP. 55% of mobile advertising are mobile search ads.
Mobile display ads	Similar to display ads shown on a desktop or laptop, mobile image ads may be interstitial or banner ads. • Interstitial are full-page adverts and tend to get a higher click-through rate • Banner ads are small ads that sit across the top or bottom of the mobile or tablet screen • Mobile display ads are increasingly rich media, such as interactive games or video messages. • Native advertising, or ads embedded into website content, are also very popular on mobile.
App promotion ads	Advertising within mobile apps includes: native advertising within the content of the app; display banners; video content; interstitial advertisements (ads across the entire page of the app); and rich media, including games.
Call-only ads	If you want to drive traffic to call your business, then 'call-only' advertisements work well. They are set up so that people can call your business directly from their smartphone. The phone number of your business is embedded in the ad and when a consumer clicks on it, a direct line to the business pops up.

TEXT MESSAGE ADVERTISING: BE CAREFUL — Promoting your business by text can be risky. You must get the explicit consent of the person that you are texting and be sure that the information you provide is highly relevant to their needs. You must record and keep demonstrable proof that this consent has been received.

One local restaurant, now closed, collected mobile numbers through their Internet booking service and then sent random texts at random hours to their customers. Some of those customers were once-off diners who had no loyalty to the restaurant. There was no way to unsubscribe.

The way people feel about their mobile phones is quite different to their PCs or even tablets. Texts are usually only sent by intimate acquaintances. If, as a business, you assume that intimacy when it does not exist in the mind of the customer, then you are imposing. It is possible to trigger negative emotions in customers about your brand if you assume an intimacy to which you are not entitled. Also, the fines on businesses for sending notifications, without the recipient's consent are very high under data protection legislation. Individuals can also seek compensation in the courts. (For guidelines on advertising, see the ASAI Code of Standards for Advertising and Marketing Communications in Ireland at www.asai.ie.)

Geo-location advertising

According to research by the PEW Institute, 77% of adults owning smartphones use them to find information based on their current location. Location-based advertising provides particular infor-mation in real-time about what is happening in a locality.

Smartphones or tablets can identify a person's location and, if they are happy to share that information, attract location-specific advertisements to the device. When you tie geo-location to customer behaviour, you get a fantastic way to market to people harnessing their behavioural patterns.

Geo-location advertising can also be used to provide customers, who have previously expressed interest in your business, with coupons, special gifts and flash sales.

Both Google My Business listings and Google Maps are useful tools and channels for geo-location advertising.

Behavioural advertising

Take a closer look at the advertisements that target you online. They reflect your interests, online behaviour and browser history. As an online advertiser, you can target customers according to their interests and behaviour. This type of advertising is interest-based or online behavioural advertising.

Interest-based advertising follows your customers' online behaviour with 'cookies' and, without recording personal details, it can aggregate demographic profiles, interests and lifestyles by tracking the websites they visit. (A 'cookie' is a small piece of data sent from a website and stored on the user's computer by the user's web browser while the user is browsing.) For example, if a person is a sailing enthusiast and visits various sailing goods websites, interest-based advertisement will show him or her ads relating to sailing gear, chandlery and sailing courses.

Your business can benefit from interest-based advertising by working with aggregators who help you place your ads into the right niches. Using AdSense, consumers can also specify what types of advertisements they would like or prefer not to receive.

Remarketing
Have you ever noticed that after you look at a particular product or service online, you see adverts from that service provider long after you left their site? This is called remarketing, which targets people who have interacted and are familiar with your website.

Sophisticated remarketing enables you to show ads tailored to the specific interests of people who visited your site. If, for example, your customer explores a particular deal on your website, you can then put that deal in front of them again as they enter other websites or search engines. Many online retailers put forward the exact clothing items a customer has looked at in a remarketing display advertisement that follows them from website. Under the privacy and data protection rules, you must let users of your website know, within your privacy policy, that you may use data collected through cookies for remarketing purposes.

BONUS – GETTING LONG-TERM BENEFITS FROM ONLINE ADVERTISING

GET PERMISSION TO (RE)MARKET TO VISTORS TO YOUR WEBSITE IN THE FUTURE.

If as a result of your online advertisement, a person clicks through to your website, 'capture' them with a free trial or promotion code in return for their email address and consent to market to that person in the future and possibly attract business from them. (To comply with data protection, keep a record of their consent.)

CHOOSE YOUR TIMING CAREFULLY.

If you are a small business, you may find online advertising too expensive long term. You may prefer to use it in short bursts, for example to drive traffic to your website for a promotion. You can also use online advertising to test the popularity of certain keywords and keyword phrases among your target audience. Test ideas, concepts and keywords, and find out which ones attract most attention.

ONCE YOUR ADVERTISING STOPS, THEN YOUR STREAM OF CUSTOMERS STOPS.

Online advertising works when you have the budget and it stops when you don't, unlike print advertising, which has a longer shelf life. (Videos are an exception). So, you have to work to harness the maximum benefits from your online advertising while you are doing it, to derive some longer-term benefit.

AT A GLANCE   CHAPTER FIVE

Online advertising is generally paid for and it is the fastest growing method of advertising on the planet.

Customer insights, keywords and target customer segments are critical information pieces that you need to have in place before you approach online advertising. The in-depth research that I recommend in **Chapters 1** and 2 must be done first.

Blendtec's use of video shows how small businesses can achieve phenomenal results online. This is a simple, illustration of how highly effective online advertising works. Look at your business: how can you show it to best effect in words, in images and in video?

In all of your advertising you should aim to be informative, problem-solving and/or provide value to the consumer. So, be outward looking. Work out what will impress your prospective customers. Test various iterations of your advertisements and see which ones work best.

Social media advertising is growing in popularity. If Facebook earned over $26 billion in advertising revenue in 2016, it must be delivering for business. What makes social media advertising particularly attractive is your ability to target customers forensically – right down to their interests and behaviours.

A challenge for all businesses is to ensure that you comply with data protection laws as set out by the EU in the GDPR (General Data Protection Regulation) – see **Appendix A** – which can include getting and recording consumers' explicit consent for using their personal data in direct marketing and drawing their attention to remarketing activities in your privacy policy.

CHAPTER SIX
EMAIL MARKETING

What is great about the Salt House Inn in Provincetown, Massachusetts? What is scintillating about Noshon.it? What is fascinating about Buzzfeed? All three regularly run fantastic email campaigns. We can learn something useful from each of their approaches.

You might imagine that with all of the social media interactive capability available to us, email marketing might be going out of fashion, but permission email marketing continues to be one of the most used and successful digital marketing tools. If you follow the new rules of email marketing, as well as, of course, the legal requirements around personal data, your business has the opportunity to build real relationships with loyal customers.

According to Natalie Chan of Outbrain, 44% of promotional email recipients have purchased products they saw first in an email marketing campaign. This statistic shows the power email has to convert prospects to customers.

The key is cracking the design, content and personalisation emails. In the **Introduction**, I emphasised that customers don't want noise in their inbox. Consumers will revolt against digital marketing canon-fire. They want calm, targeted solutions and a road map to happiness.

Email content

The best email marketing is driven by relevant content supported by excellent design, and technology that can deliver your message to the right market segments. Your aim should be to focus on the human side of email marketing.

CASE STUDY BUZZFEED TO 650+ MILLION PEOPLE — Buzzfeed is one of the best when it comes to email marketing. It provides shareable news, broken down into well-defined segments, to a global audience of more than 200 million people. Below is a good example of a Buzzfeed sign-up/opt-in email sent to parents and prospective parents.

"Hey Parents: Buzzfeed has a newsletter just for you. By people with kids, for people with kids.

Who it's for: Parents or parents-to-be looking for recipes, crafts, and parenting hacks – or even just a laugh about what it's like to raise another human.

What you'll get: Brilliant tips that will make every day easier, from the earliest days of pregnancy to the very end of the school year. DIY projects and recipes your kids will love. Special ways to spend time together. Inspired activities to keep them busy. Real talk about what being a parent is really like, hilarious proof that it's OK not to have all the answers and much more!

When you'll get it: Wednesday and Saturday.

Enter your email address to sign up now!"*

The audience insights discussed in **Chapter 1** are clearly visible in the communication by Buzzfeed to the various segments of their market. Their communication is a well thought-out strategy and with an audience of over 650 million people, their strategy is working.

FIGURE 6.1 — LESSONS FROM BUZZFEED

Relevant

Don't inundate people with irrelevant junk mail. Tap into your audience's interests, desires, needs, and help them to be better, happier, more informed, amused. Buzzfeed manages this by honing in on the topics that people really can relate to. I mentioned emotional triggers early on and your email marketing should include content that attracts people at an emotional level. Look at Buzzfeed.

Easy to read

Great design is an extremely powerful tool to help readers focus on the information that you want them to take in. In your email, list, in order of importance, the content that you want to pass to consumers, making sure the top three messages are most visible to the reader. While numbered lists may seem a hackneyed way to present content, they do make content easy to read.

Focus on the design of your emails and news- letters, to make sure that they are im-pactful, preferably understated and visually appealing. Sometimes, a particular style of business needs an 'in your face' presentation of information. That's the exception, rather than the rule. Most good email marketing is presented in a calm and restrained way. Take a look at salthouseinn.com and their newsletter.

Responsive

You want people to respond to your email. It might be an offer, a discount, an invitation or an opportunity. Encourage people to opt-in by providing an obvious call to action. A call to action is an invitation by you to your customer to do something: call us, email us, sign up for our newsletter, buy with discount, or buy six and get one free, and so on. Aim to build trust. Don't hide in the legal lines how people can opt-out or unsubscribe from your emails. Check out how this is done well by Noshon.it.

FIGURE 6.2 — SEVEN WAYS TO IMPROVE YOUR
EMAIL MARKETING

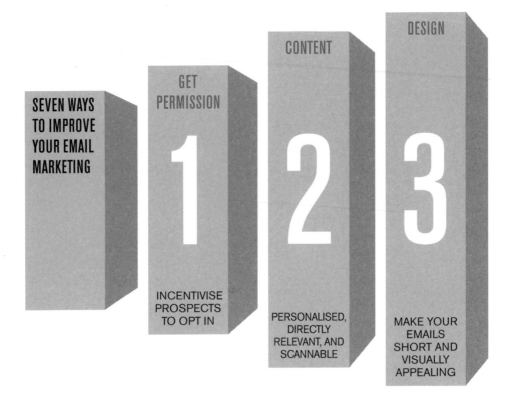

Get permission

It is assumed in this chapter about email marketing that you have the permission of the recipients. So, to maximise the benefits when it comes to email marketing, you want your target customers to volunteer their contact information and interests so you can write to them legitimately. (Again, segmentation will be useful for such targeting.) Once you know who you want to target, you want them to choose to engage with you, and having them opt in to your emails and newsletters is a great way to do that. Your invitation to join your mailing list can be in an advertisement, an online article or blog post as well as on your website.

Approach this request for emails in an honest way. Explain that you want to provide subscribers with useful and relevant information on what would interest them most. Have a strong tagline to drive home the benefits that opt-in provides, and offer an incentive to people for signing up. You will find your persona profiling useful here – you will know exactly what motivates the people you want to attract and this enables you to steer the online conversation in a way that says 'we get you' (see **Chapter 1**).

When you invite people to join your mailing list, make sure to describe in detail what your subscribers will get and how often. People need to know what to expect from you, whether it's a once-off promotional offer or a daily newsletter. Be upfront and allow people to choose whether your planned communication suits them or not. You can also give people the option of weekly or monthly communication, which again builds up trust in your business model.

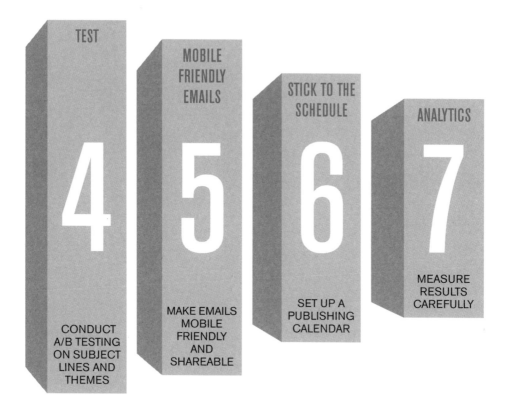

A WORD ABOUT SPAM The General Data Protection Regulation (GDPR) — In force from 25 May 2018, and designed to protect privacy rights, the GDPR introduces more stringent data protection and compliance requirements for businesses across the EU, and indeed for organisations worldwide collecting and using the personal data of individuals that are EU resident.

Consumer consent to receiving emails cannot be ambiguous – there must be clear record of it having been given, and this must be renewed every 12 months. Organisations must ensure that their record-keeping is fully up to date and open to inspection by the Regulator.

GDPR legislation makes consent for processing personal data harder. The consent obtained from each individual that receives an email from you must be unambiguous and you have to be able to prove that you received permission. Consent has to be gained retrospectively for people who receive your email, and haven't expressly consented – by ticking a box, for example.

If you collect email addresses for some other purpose, then using those emails for marketing purposes is illegal. You don't have permission to use email addresses for marketing purposes unless you specifically ask for consent from the individual. Otherwise, you may find yourself subject to the strict penalties available under data protection legislation, including the prospect of being sued by the individuals involved.

Start with an honest, up-front and human approach to prospective subscribers to your emails and newsletters and they are more likely to respect you and your brand. Include an obvious 'UNSUBSCRIBE' link in every email.

Content

You are already aware that today's successful digital marketing is all about specific, relevant, useful, entertaining, high-quality content. It's important to make that content readable. Your email has to be easy to read, pithy and interesting. Good marketing people today know that their tech-savvy subscribers are not interested in unclear email communications.

Aim to be:

1. Human

2. Personal

3. Informal

A positive reaction to your newsletter's content will help your search engine ranking and drive business to your website and online store.

Design templates

Design of your emails and newsletters is paramount. You will find many excellent email marketing software providers online providing effective email marketing templates, design options, image and brand logo uploading, and location maps and also registration pages for signing people up to the newsletter (for example, Createsend.ie).

Email marketing software also helps you to manage your distribution database and most provide tracking information so that you can see how many people engaged with your email campaign by opening and clicking on offers. Take a look at Constant Contact, Campaign Monitor, Zoho Campaigns, and Mailchimp.

We have discussed avoiding clutter and people being overloaded with information. If you don't send a well-designed thoughtfully arranged email that contains relevant information, then it could actually be seen as spam by recipients. Low-quality design work will not attract a wide audience; there are too many competing priorities.

Even if you use email marketing software, and appealing templates, you may want to get a designer to help you format the email at the start – to ensure that it looks professional and contemporary.

It's not that difficult to produce a high-quality email. Modern email majors on beautiful imagery, plenty of white space and an uncluttered layout.

CASE STUDY — THE SALTHOUSE INN — The Salthouse Inn team located in Provincetown, Massachusetts use exceptional design to market their property.

Branding is very important to the Salthouse Inn staff. The brand reflects the ambition of the inn to create a calm, holiday feel for their target audience. The imagery used is gorgeous. Reading their website or online newsletter invokes a sense of relaxation and makes this inn a compelling holiday destination choice. The Salthouse Inn newsletter appeals to people seeking a calm, relaxed and visually beautiful holiday. It meets the needs of a swathe of holiday-makers seeking to escape their cluttered, hectic and over-stimulated city existence to a simpler, calmer and more stylish break.

What's most instructive is how Salthouse Inn convey this image using their email marketing. The aim of their carefully produced newsletters and emails is to send a feeling of calm through to potential vacationers. This is one of those magical occasions when digital marketing – this time in the form of an eNewsletter – reaches the soul of its readers.

Test

If you have more than one good marketing concept, headline or offer, why not test them out to find which most engages your audience? Many of the email marketing services mentioned above allow you to test out various headlines and run the campaigns that achieve the greatest level of interest.

The most important aspect of your email is your subject line. Some headlines attract more attention than others. It is hard to know which is better unless you do an objective test. You can test subject lines using a number of different varieties or calls-to-action.

FIGURE 6.3 — SEVEN ELEMENTS TO CONSIDER WHEN
TESTING EMAILS

SEVEN ELEMENTS TO CONSIDER WHEN TESTING EMAILS

A/B testing is exactly that: testing between an A choice or a B choice. (Don't test too many variables or you will have difficulty working out which are more successful.)

Test like a scientist:
• control A
• variable B
• hypothesis

Send test emails at the same time. Time of day is also an important test factor in sending emails. People are receptive to types of emails at certain times of day so try to find out what time is best for your audience.

Read data as observations:
• open rate
• click through rate (CTR) to links
• response to call to action (CTA)

Your total database should be at least 1,000 and you should use 10% for testing.

Wait 24 to 48 hours before making a choice between email versions.

Be real: tests must provide statistically significant results and this means that there must be high enough numbers (e.g. at least 50 each for A and B tests) surveyed to make the results realistic.

Act on your results: choose the most statistically successful email.

Mobile-friendly emails

According to research from e-Dialog, 41% of Europeans and 63% of Americans will close an email that is not easy to read on their mobile phones. Most people now access the Internet using a smartphone or tablet. You must format your emails so that they are easily accessed via mobile devices. Send test emails or use a testing program to make sure that your emails look great on all screen types.

Stick to the schedule

When you tell your readers you'll be contacting them on a schedule, you have to honour that commitment. If you go a number of months without sending a newsletter, your subscribers are likely to forget that they opted-in. They could delete your email and consign it to spam when they get one out of the blue.

It is easy to keep a publishing schedule. Decide on the themes of each email communication in advance and link each to your business objectives. Involve members of your sales team in the design of the calls-to-action.

The Irish Fairy Door Company regularly emails 200,000 people and littler people who own fairy doors. Not only does the company generate great delight and unswerving brand loyalty with those emails, they also get the opportunity to keep subscribers informed of new developments and accessories from the Irish Fairy Door Company.

Analytics

Most email marketing services give you free statistics so you can easily see how many emails are opened, shared and achieve clickthroughs to websites.

The email marketing service will also monitor and manage the people who unsubscribe from your email. This will help give you a strong indication of the quality of your data. If you receive a high number of people unsubscribing, then you have to do something different. If you are using a segmentation model, you should be able to analyse which segments your email marketing appeals to most.

Customer feedback

It is a good idea to send emails to customers requesting their feedback. It will help to improve your service and customer support. Remember: less is more. A few, succinct questions and a gracious 'thank you' will achieve results.

FIGURE 6.4 — TOP 10 SUCCESS FACTORS FOR AN EMAIL CAMPAIGN
(SOURCE: REPORT BY HOWLING MAD 2014)

1 SUBJECT LINE

2 QUALITY OF DATA

3 SEGMENT SELECTION

4 HUMAN CREATIVITY

5 EMAIL AESTHETICS / DESIGN

6 TIME OF DAY

7 RENDERING ON MULTIPLE DEVICES

8 DELIVERABILITY INFRASTRUCTURE

9 EMAIL SERVICE PROVIDER

10 LIST SIZE

AT A GLANCE   CHAPTER SIX

Email marketing has remained the single most popular form of digital marketing. It is a way of communicating with current and potential customers. Your main aim is to get permission, explicit consent, from your customers and prospects to send them emails. These emails often take the form of newsletters or news updates – or simply branded emails, in the form of a letter.

Your first thought should be the content of your email. It must be relevant to the needs and motivations of your customers. Prioritise your messages and list them in order. Make sure that the most important messages are also the ones that are highlighted. Always have a call-to-action – asking people to respond, or buy or avail of an offer. You have to incentivise people to follow up.

Remember: today it is crucial to humanise the customer and so your emails should be personalised for the recipient. Email marketing services and software will allow you to personalise your emails efficiently.

It is important, when signing people up, to describe in detail what they will get from you. In order to target your information to the right people, try to get relevant information from them about what they are interested in, so that you can design your email specifically for them. Then test a number of emails, including headings, to find out which ones yield the best results.

Finally, personal email addresses are just that – personal. Always be aware and market within bounds of the General Data Protection Regulation (GDPR) and keep demonstrable, accurate and current records of all those individuals who opt in and opt out.

The 'Internet of Things' is a major emerging trend and mobile phone apps are making it possible. Use your mobile phone to turn off your house alarm and turn on your central heating. Take payments from customers on the go with Sumup. Catch a mytaxi in your near vicinity and follow the taxi's progress as it travels the route to collect you. Apps improve your digital marketing performance when they make life easier for the consumer.

Apt and appropriate apps

In the **Introduction** we encountered consumer power and the second digital revolution a key aspect of which is consumers' fascination with and desire for any technology that makes their life easier. Apps facilitate that and if you can design an app for your business that simplifies things for your customer, then they are probably with you.

You may think that apps are just for big business, but as the cost of developing them comes down, small businesses use apps more and more to generate sales leads and to provide some service or education to customers. As you would when developing a new website, look at cost-effective, off-the-shelf options provided by companies such as Phorest before commissioning a more bespoke version.

CASE STUDY mytaxi (originally branded as Hailo before the company's merger with Daimler's mytaxi) is an app that enables the user to order a taxi to their exact location in two quick steps. Taxi fare is charged to a credit card that you supply and that is stored in the app. The geo-mapping facility allows you to track the taxi as it travels to collect you. You even get the name and mobile number of the driver who is picking you up.

mytaxi is now a European-wide business operating in nine countries and 50 cities. However, the original app was not started by big business; Hailo was founded by three London cabbies and three online entrepreneurs.

Within two years, the Hailo brand had raised over £100 million in investment funding. The key to the success of Hailo was that it began as a useful tool for taxi drivers, before it was launched to consumers. It succeeded in making the taxi driver's job more efficient and more effective. When they launched to consumers, Hailo already had hundreds of drivers set up.

FIGURE 7.1 — HOW MYTAXI WINS CUSTOMERS BY APP

LOCAL   INVALUABLE   PARTNERSHIP

Local

Apps work best when they apply to people on a local scale. mytaxi may now be a European-wide business, but the app works wherever the customer is based. It involves signing up local taxi drivers and matching them to local customers.

Invaluable

One of the great successes of Hailo/mytaxi came from the buy-in from taxi drivers. It helps them to manage their business more efficiently. Your app will only be downloaded and retained if it is truly useful to your prospective audiences and of course to your business.

Partnership

If you are planning to develop an app, then partnerships are important. Over time, if your app becomes as successful as mytaxi, you may have to develop a business case to get financial backing. You may link with other influencers in your market space to develop valuable content within the app. Most importantly, you will also have to partner with the right app suppliers or developers to make sure that you produce an app that looks fantastic and performs really efficiently. Do your research and only work with app providers that are well-established and have an excellent track record in your sector.

FIGURE 7.2 — SIX ELEMENTS TO CONSIDER WHEN DEVELOPING AN APP FOR YOUR BUSINESS

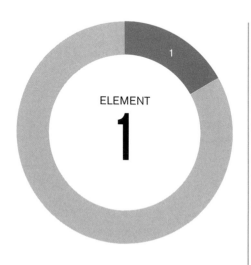

ELEMENT
1

ADDRESS CLIENT NEEDS

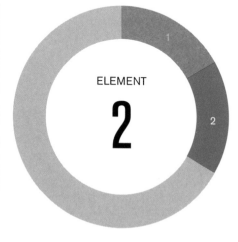

ELEMENT
2

A USEFUL TOOL

FIGURE 7.2 CONT. — SIX ELEMENTS TO CONSIDER WHEN DEVELOPING
AN APP FOR YOUR BUSINESS

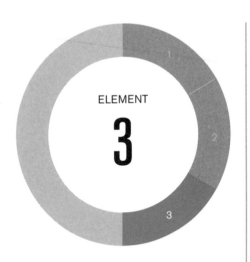

ELEMENT

3

CUSTOMERS & PROSPECTS

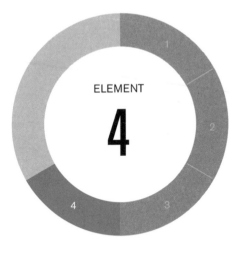

ELEMENT

4

LIFESTYLE

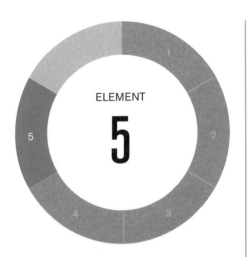

ELEMENT

5

ENTERTAINMENT / GAMING

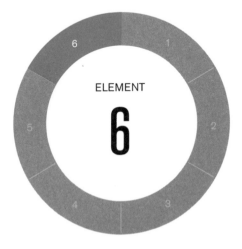

ELEMENT

6

EDUCATION

Address client needs

The early chapters of this book emphasised researching the customer perspective – when you understand and characterise your customers in detail, then you can develop new ways to satisfy their needs and provide solutions to their challenges. It is from this research that the idea and design for a useful app could evolve.

HOWTH HAVEN

HOWTH HAVEN BEAUTY SALON IN NORTH COUNTY DUBLIN USES BOOKING SOFTWARE BY PHOREST.COM. FOR A MONTHLY SUB-SCRIPTION FEE, THE SALON HAS ACCESS TO A CUSTOMISABLE APP THAT ENABLES CLIENTS TO BROWSE AND BOOK BEAUTY TREATMENTS AND PROVIDE FEEDBACK ON THE SERVICE. A SALON OWNER CAN USE THE PHOREST APP TO MONITOR CLIENT BOOKINGS ON THEIR MOBILE PHONE, ORDER NEW STOCK, ROSTER STAFF AND PRODUCE REPORTS.

Useful for customers – not a sales tool

Thousands of small businesses now offer apps that are useful tools for their customers. Your priority should be to create a tool that is time-saving, efficient and convenient, and not a tool that merely flogs your goods or services. Aim to prioritise customer needs and provide an app, like mytaxi, that adds value in the life of the customer. Mary Berry has a baking app to accompany her baking books. Dulux created a visualiser app to help you choose the right paint.

Customers and prospects

Apps for customers
You will find that you distribute your app firstly among your existing customer base. As I outlined above, if the app is useful, customers will use it and, importantly, will pass it on to other prospective customers. An app should help to promote loyalty to your brand and reinforce the reasons why customers become loyal in the first place.

Apps for prospective customers
Attracting new customers to an app requires some advertising spend. (Online advertising is discussed in **Chapter 5**.) Your app should be included on your advertising, website, business cards and marketing material.

Don't expect your app to achieve high downloads immediately. Prepare for a slow but gradual success – first, among customers and then among prospects.

Lifestyle

There are thousands of apps that support the desire to have a better life or lifestyle: weight control, fitness, managing stress and pursuing hobbies. There are a number of social media apps that help to keep people in touch. Travel apps keep people informed of local events and 'must see' events, and the advent of geo-location technology, as discussed in **Chapter 1**, connects online services to the world in real-time.

Entertainment and gaming

Gaming is a useful way to help people to develop new skills in an entertaining way. It may suit your business model to produce an app that entertains and informs at the same time. The Blue September campaign created the gaming app 'Keepy Uppy' to help raise funds for the Men's Cancer Alliance.

Education

Apps are an invaluable tool for teaching and learning. By now, most parents have downloaded an app to help educate their child. In your business, is there an app that could help to promote your services and educate your customers at the same time? The children's school learning tool Jolly Phonics has a Letter Sounds app designed to accompany the Jolly Phonics academic books that children use all over the world.

There are also productivity, news, photo and video apps that help people keep up with news and develop new skills. The Sims IVF Mind/Body app links education with lifestyle management to help people understand more about fertility testing and treatment and to prepare for their in vitro fertilisation journey. Apps are also an excellent way to help people to understand a professional service in more detail and in a creative way.

AT A GLANCE   CHAPTER SEVEN

The 'Internet of Things' is an emerging trend that will see mobile phone apps used more and more. From turning on the heating to booking a restaurant, apps are pervasive. Hailo went from start-up to stellar with their phenomenal mobile app.

Mobile apps are completely consumer-focused. Start with the needs of your best customers and build an app to meet their requirements. Apps are not just for big businesses; they also work for SMEs.

If you can come up with an app that makes the life of your customers easier, then you will earn their loyalty. Your aim is to provide an app that focuses less on sales and more on supporting the customer – sales and loyalty, of course, are the ultimate results.

Apps are a great way of providing entertainment and education. In this way, apps are a useful tool for building brand awareness or for highlighting an important cause like the Men's Cancer Alliance.

Don't expect your app to take off immediately – it is usually a slow-burn. First, you market it to your existing customers. Then you may need paid advertising to build awareness in a wider target audience.

When you spend money on digital marketing media, you want to see your business appear right at the top of a search engine results page (SERP). Good search engine optimisation (SEO) management helps you to be seen by your target customers. The biggest challenge for any online business is how to attract customers to their store online. Often that means attracting the attention of online search engines. How do you start to achieve a good SEO ranking?

SEO defined

SEO is the set of processes that help your website achieve a high ranking on SERPs for popular search engines such as Google, Yahoo and Bing. Your search engine ranking, both off- and on-page, can be greatly improved if you use SEO techniques.

There is no agreement on which is more successful – off- or on-page SEO. There is agreement, however, that both are essential. Off-page SEO techniques help you to achieve a high rank on search engines and good quality on-page SEO helps to keep you there.

Off-page SEO

Off-page SEO refers to particular techniques used to improve your website's performance on a SERP that are not controlled by how you format your site, but instead by the popularity of your site and other third-party sites linking to yours. When another website links to a page on your website, that's called an in-bound link. The more in-bound links you have, the better.

Off-page SEO includes:

• Articles and blogs linking to your site
• PR
• Advertising

• Posts on forums about your site
• Directory listings
• RSS feed aggregators.

On-page SEO

In **Chapter 2**, I mentioned organic SERP results. On-page or organic search engine optimisation means that you are in control of keeping your website high on search engine ranking lists without having to pay for such a ranking. This can be done by keeping your content fresh, formatting the text of your website to ensure that it is picked up by search engine algorithms and optimising your images and URL structures.

On-page SEO is controlled by you and the coding of your website and it includes:

• Keyword strategy, density and quality
• Meta keywords and descriptions
• Headings within your website (H1, H2, H3, etc.)
• Use of bold text to highlight key messages
• User-friendly navigation
• URL structures
• Alt tags or alternative tagging of images
• Internal links within your website
• Links to external websites
• Fast-loading pages.

CASE STUDY HAPPY KIDS MONTESSORI SCHOOL — Hannah established a new Montessori pre-school called Happy Kids in a particular suburb of Melbourne where she knew that demand for pre-school nurseries outstripped supply. She was conscious of the fact that in addition to personal recommendations, the Internet was one of the best ways to get the message out about her new Montessori school.

Hannah commissioned a new website for the Happy Kids Montessori School. The key selling point and her most important word on the website was 'Montessori'. Hanna produced carefully written website copy to illustrate how her Montessori techniques would benefit south Melbourne's children in terms of education and entertainment.

Hannah built it but they did not come. It is easy to believe that if you build a website, people will automatically come. Three months after the Happy Kids website was launched, Hannah and her web developers were shocked to find that almost no one had actually found her Happy Kids Montessori website. No calls. No emails. No contact.

They decided to do some research into why a pre-school that was needed in the local community failed to attract visitors seeking that particular service. When Hannah typed the keyword 'pre-school' into a search engine, her school did not appear in the top ten. Neither was it in the top ten for childcare or for nursery. There was work to be done on Hannah's SEO.

FIGURE 8.1 — THREE LESSONS FROM HAPPY KIDS
MONTESSORI SCHOOL

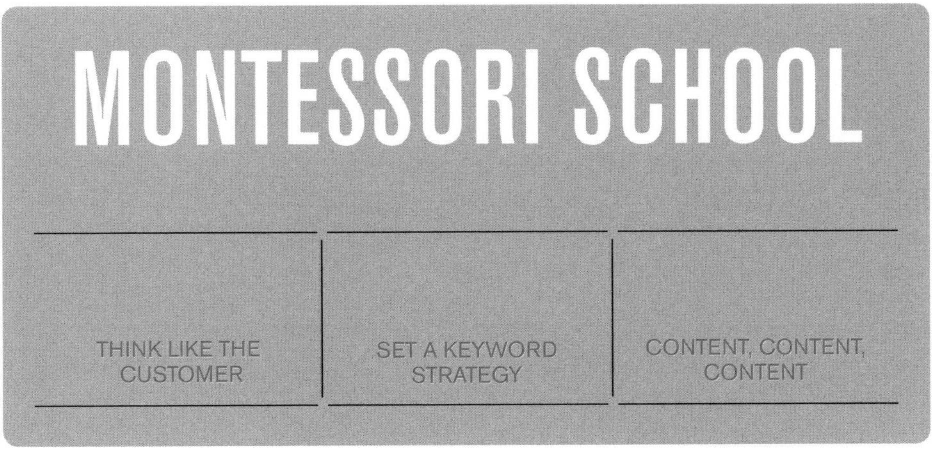

MONTESSORI SCHOOL

| THINK LIKE THE CUSTOMER | SET A KEYWORD STRATEGY | CONTENT, CONTENT, CONTENT |

Think like the customer

Hannah's first lesson was to think like a parent and not like a Montessori professional. Your mind-set has to be the same – think like the client, the prospective customer. 'Montessori' was not the first word parents considered when looking for a nursery school. In fact, Hannah's research showed that people very seldom use the word. It is cumbersome to spell, for a start. 'Pre-school', 'childcare' and 'playschool' were much more widely used.

Set a keyword strategy

This simple story, as well as our discussion in **Chapter 3**, shows the importance of having a keyword strategy for your SEO. Every person that seeks out a website uses the keyword or keyword phrase they believe will take them to content, services or goods that most fit their needs. Search engines, in turn, rank sites based on keywords and a highly sophisticated algorithm of other factors. They do not think in terms of your 'industry speak' or jargon, and prefer customer-oriented language.

Hannah discovered that when people use search engines such as Google, they use key words and phrases such as 'pre-school', 'childcare', 'nursery' or longer phrases like 'a school for my three-year-old'. Design your website keywords and phrases to be relevant to your customer. Use them in key places, such as headings, images and through-out the body of your homepage.

Google Adwords has a Keyword Planner to help you monitor and evaluate your keyword performance. It allows you to find the best keywords for your particular industry.

Search engine algorithms change very regularly and as I have said throughout the book, are very complex in their analysis of web information. Try to keep up to date with the latest search engine optimisation tools and ask your website developer to help you to keep on top of SEO requirements, so that your website doesn't lose momentum.

Content, content, content

Content is not only relevant for entertaining and informing customers, it is also critical in helping people to find your website and social media pages. Hannah had produced content relating to Montessori and the principles of childhood education. In order to improve her SEO, she could also provide articles on various aspects of childhood education, play and entertainment on her website. Rich interactive content such as games and puzzles would also be valuable. All of this content contributes to successful SEO management.

If you plan to redesign or update your website in the future, then here are six SEO building blocks you need to understand to ensure that your website is the best it can be in the marketplace.

FIGURE 8.2 — SIX BUILDING BLOCKS OF SEO

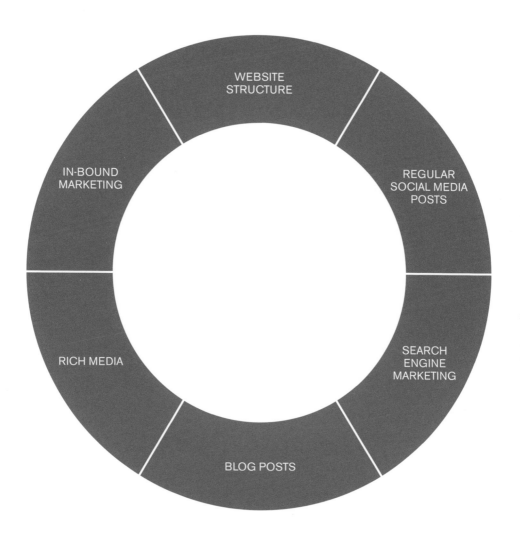

Website structure

In **Chapter 3**, we looked at the various elements that will make your website appeal to your target audience. Now we look at the elements that attract search engines, our ultimate aim being to get in front of your target audience. There are three key elements that will help you get search engine recognition:

1. Fresh content

2. Keywords

3. Headings

Fresh content

Fresh content attracts the most attention from search engines. Search engine algorithms are set up to be attracted to dynamic, topical, journalistic style content. Stagnant content is easily ignored and is not considered interesting enough to achieve first-page search status because it is not seen as current.

Content will only get the search engine's interest if it is trending and relevant. You could think of content marketing as making umbrellas available when it's raining. You have to think about what is interesting and likely to be read or viewed by a wide audience if you want to achieve high search engine rankings. Look at what is trending in your business environment – hot topics, customer's key concerns, and do some research to find out what customers really look for in your market space.

Keywords

Hannah's first lesson was to think like a parent and not like a Montessori professional. Your mindset has to be the same – think like a customer, not like a business, when writing your keywords.

Headings

When you are setting up and developing your website, you may think that you are just entering a simple heading for your homepage or a summary page for your services – think again. Websites are a sophisticated tool to attract clients and you need to know how to use them. Use your keywords strategically in headings from H1 to H2 and so forth.

Heading 1

Heading 2

Heading 3

Heading 4

Heading 5

As you can see in the illustration above, H1 Tags are the biggest and boldest headings and H5 are the smallest. They are used to define your web page information. There should only ever be one H1 on a page. The H1 tag denotes the most important information on your page. It's your main headline. It is also the information that search engines will focus on first so make that heading highly relevant to what your customer is searching for.

Social media

Regular, sustained and consistent use of social media presents infinite ways to promote your website and improve your search engine ranking. It allows you to build a loyal following, to answer customer questions directly, to talk about the progress of your business (launches, expansions, staff profiles, and expert articles) and to share customer insights and stories.

If you host a Twitter discussion and it ends up trending in your location, you have the opportunity to drive a lot more traffic to your website. If you are running a lively Facebook campaign repleat with comments about your product, again, you are more likely to pick up more website traffic and to attract the interest of search engines.

Search engine marketing (SEM)

As discussed in detail in **Chapter 5**, search engine marketing (SEM) is advertising offered by search engines. Customers who search for a particular keyword receive multiple results for their search. These results are called organic search results. In addition to those results, the person also receives SEM advertising at the top and bottom of the page that the search engine algorithms judges to be most relevant to the search.

A business can bid for search engine advertising space. Search engines such as Google and Yahoo offer space on their search engine pages for advertising campaigns relating to the subject being researched.

Blog posts

Blog posts are crucial content for your website. At first you might think that writing a blog post is too time-consuming. In reality, you probably have all the content you need; it is just a job of organising your information, cutting it down into chunks of 600–1,500 words and scheduling it.

Schedule 10 blog posts in advance, drawn from your company's PR articles, events, guides or booklets, or comment on popular topics of the day. Most people, when they go looking around their company for information, find more than 10 easy-to-access pieces of information that they can easily write up into blog posts.

To start, create a blog in WordPress or Blogger – both systems make blogging easy, but there are many blogging platforms available.

In-bound marketing

If you want your website to achieve optimisation from a search engine perspective, set up campaigns and initiatives that will draw people in. That means setting the stage for in-bound marketing, or getting people to contact you, rather than you contacting them.

In-bound marketing is all about getting leads. When you get approval to provide further marketing information to a client, then the person who has come to your website has 'opted-in.' Where possible, try to get in-bound leads – leads that are initiated by a potential customer who goes to your site. Inbound-leads are always more likely to result in sales than out-bound contact, contact initiated by you.

Inbound leads can be generated in a number of ways:

IN-BOUND LINKS When another website links to a page on your website, that's called an in-bound link. The more in-bound links you have, the better. These links mean that you are meeting the needs of customers in your market and search engines see this as positive.

CONTACT NUMBER on every page of your site.

CONTACT ME BUTTON on every page of your site. Behind this button is a form that requests a name, phone number and query from the customer. Only include this button if you will respond quickly.

OPT-IN FORM OR SUBSCRIBE BUTTONS on your site's landing page so that people can follow your newsletter or get your latest marketing information by email. Include a well-thought out punch-line to show the benefits of opting in, as discussed in **Chapter 6**.

PR Get other bloggers, commentators or PR people to comment on your business and what you offer.

SOCIAL MEDIA As we have seen, social media campaigns build brand profile and strengthen your SEO.

Rich media

As discussed in **Chapter 3**, games, video or other rich media can improve the quality of your search engine status. Research puts rich media as the most important trend for the future and so you will find that the most successful websites use rich media extensively.

Webinars

If you want to conduct a workshop or conference for people on some aspect of your business, you can use a website like Webinarjam.com to create an online webinar. Such tools are easy and cost-effective to run online.

When webinars are used properly, they are extraordinarily efficient and cost effective in helping you to communicate with a wide audience. No one has to travel, it's low cost and the entire event can be saved and watched online after the event. If your webinar is topical and provides your audience with new ideas, skills or action plans, then this is the type of content that will keep your website fresh and interesting.

AT A GLANCE   CHAPTER EIGHT

Search engine optimisation (SEO) is about being on the first SERP or search engine results page of Google, Bing or Yahoo, for example.

There are a number of ways that you can ensure that you are top of the search-engine ranking for your business. How you structure your website is important. Fresh and relevant content, customer focused keywords, longer keyword phrases and properly labeled images are important to attract search engine crawlers. Google AdWords has a keyword planner facility to help you evaluate your search engine ranking on certain key words.

A combination of online advertising through AdWords, attention grabbing social media campaigns and rich media all highlight the dynamism of a brand and again, they attract the attention of search engines.

Aim to integrate all your online marketing activity, so that you can create a unified approach to your search engine success.

A key to SEO success is in-bound marketing, which involves drawing people voluntarily to your website and social media pages. When people come to your website via links on other sites and blogs, this is rated favourably by search engines. The rationale is that if people are referred to your site by bloggers, journalists and other websites, your site must be rated.

You have your digital assets (website, social media, advertising, and email marketing) and you are aware of what it takes to achieve search engine optimisation. Now it is time to convert the leads that you have attracted to your website into actual sales.

CHAPTER NINE
CONVERTING LEADS

By this point you have learned about developing and getting the most from your digital media assets attracting leads. The last two chapters of this book now bring this information together to help you convert these leads to sales.

When it comes to converting online leads into sales, there are three critical elements that you have to take care of:

RESPONSE You have to respond to those leads while they are red hot.

EXPERIENTIAL Create such a positive buying experience that customers just say "wow".

OPERATIONS Focus on the smooth and efficient execution of sales orders to keep customers happy.

Companies that succeed in digital marketing put customers first; arranging their communication processes and marketing around their customers' needs to achieve the critical edge.

You have the leads. You have the customer's attention. They arrive at your site, they subscribe to your blog, they watch your YouTube video and they are open to doing business. The power is in your hands. How do you then convert these leads into revenue?

CASE STUDY 123.IE — 123.ie provides all types of insurance cover from car and health, to pet and life assurance. The mantra of 123.ie is to offer great value insurance to customers and with exceptional customer care. The company, whose motto is 'Simple is Smarter', is proud to say that 95% of 123.ie customers would recommend the company to a friend.

Marketing activity at 123.ie is structured into two teams. One team drives traffic to the website to generate leads and the second team works on converting those leads into customers.

123.ie has set up a live chat for customers, along with a phone number that is on every page of the website. Their services are available from 8am to 8pm. This allows 123.ie to instantly respond to customer leads. The aim is to make their service available when it suits the customer.

123.ie's approach is highly successful because they want to make it easy for their customer to do business online with them. When a top website development agency simplified the online sign-up process down to five steps, the 123.ie team was not satisfied. "We wanted the process to be done in 3 steps – we want to make it as easy as 123".

(Source: Padraig O'Neill, Head of Marketing, 123.ie)

TEAM ONE: DRIVE TRAFFIC	✓	TEAM TWO: CONVERT TO SALES	✓
Email		Phone calls	
Advertising		Email and live chat	
SEO		Web design	
		Upselling	

FIGURE 9.1 — THREE LESSONS FROM 123.IE

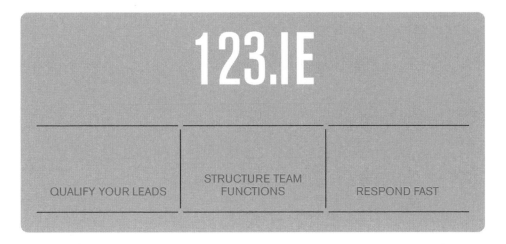

Qualify your leads

In traditional sales, businesses often spend a lot of time working on a sales pitch, matching the offering to the customer's needs, making sure that the company can satisfy those needs and also qualifying the lead – making sure that the customer fits with the business.

Online sales are different and yet, qualifying the lead and making sure that it is a good fit for your business is still important. You need to weed out time-wasters, dud-leads and cranks. Face the fact that there are people online who will send you queries that just cannot be satisfied by your business model. Qualify your leads.

How do you manage leads like this?

Carefully examine the sources of your sales requests and customer queries – is it through Facebook, customer request forms or directly by phone or by email? Find a way to qualify your leads electronically, so that only those with a bona fide enquiry come through to you.

Take the customer request form, for example. Most website developers provide a general information request form for websites, and this form requests basic information such as name, email address, as well as space for more information from the customer. Many companies use this form to qualify leads by asking a further layer of questions. The key questions that you need answered are: is this person a decision-maker/potential buyer, can they afford your product or service and do they really want to engage with your company or are they just enquiring?

Here are some questions that you can ask:

Are you an existing customer or a new customer?

What particular product/ service are you interested in? (Provide drop-down menu to assist the customer.)

What information are you looking for? (Provide drop-down menu to assist the customer.)

"The best managers have been and always will be problem solvers."

RICHARD BRANSON

Clear team functions

Make sure that there is someone on your team who has responsibility for and who can handle leads. This person is the business 'go-getter'. They should have sales targets for lead conversion from online sources. It should be their role to follow-up and work with people who enquire online.

Respond quickly

We can learn a lot from the 123.ie approach to responding to customers – availability outside of business hours and the multiple ways to contact the organisation (live chat, email and phone service) will work to ensure you won't miss a lead. Unlike 123.ie, however, many businesses are dropping the ball when it comes to re-sponding to customer leads online. Here's how:

THE PARABLE OF THE ICE-CREAM SHOP — An ice-cream shop opens up in the middle of a village. There are signs around the village pointing the way to the shop. Advertisements appear in the local paper. There is a large sign outside the door. All paths lead to this brightly lit, super-modern ice-cream parlour.

You can't resist. You go in. You say to the lady behind the counter, "I'm interested in the pistachio – may I have a taste?"

The person behind the ice-cream counter responds, "I'll get back to you in 31.5 hours".

36 hours is the typical amount of time it takes for a business to respond to its online customers by email (according to the Eptica 2017 Customer Conversations Study).

Customers want an immediate response to their enquiries. If you do get back to a customer within five minutes, there is a reasonable chance that they are still in the buying zone – at their computer, near a phone, ready to respond. However, after half an hour, the potential customer may have decided your business is too slow, left the scene and completed a transaction with your competitor. In fact, research suggests that if you don't answer an enquiry within five minutes, you are likely to have lost the lead.

FIGURE 9.2 — HOW SHOULD A BUSINESS RESPOND?

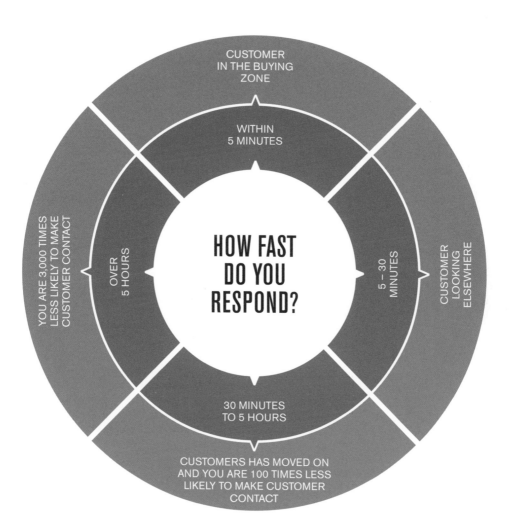

In an article on Forbes.com, Ken Krogue explains why companies waste 71% of their internet leads because they are not set up to respond within the timeframe required by their customers. Think about it: all that money invested in driving business to your website is wasted if the leads cannot be captured and followed up.

USE ATTRIBUTION MODELLING

HELP PEOPLE TO BUY

TEST EVERYTHING

FIGURE 9.3 — SIX WAYS TO CONVERT LEADS

Test everything

If you want to make sure that your system works, test everything as if you are a customer.

The 123.ie marketing team is passionate about testing both process and messaging. In fact, 10% of the marketing budget is devoted to testing how customers respond to media, creative, email and website platforms. People are regularly invited to test the purchase cycle and encouraged to comment on every stage of the process. The process is continually refined and refined until it is simple, seamless and can be transacted in as short a time-frame as possible.

Not only are people invited to test out the website and the ease of the purchase process, all digital messaging sent out by the company is also tested. Subject lines, calls-to-action, key messages and timing are elements of email campaigns that are tested. Timing is a particularly critical element. Within your target market, there are times when your prospective customers might be receptive to an email from you and times when they definitely are not. Testing will uncover the best times for contact.

KNOW THE COST TO ACQUIRE A CUSTOMER

UPSELL

REMARKET

Know the cost to acquire a customer

It costs you money to acquire a new customer through promotion, marketing and other resources. Every lead that you get, every expression of interest in your company should be followed up to bring down the cost-to-acquire figure. When a business doesn't respond to online leads, the cost to acquire customers becomes far too high.

Include an estimate of the cost to acquire each new customers as a KPI for the whole business, not just as part of the marketing or brand spend. It makes sense in today's digital world world, where so many new customers are acquired online, that online investment should be sales driven and assessed.

TOTAL MARKETING & SALES SPEND ÷ NUMBER OF NEW CUSTOMERS = COST TO ACQUIRE A CUSTOMER

To increase the value of your leads generated by online or digital marketing, set targets:

- Aim to reduce the cost-to-acquire each customer by upping the number of customers you get for your online spend.
- Incentivise your sales and marketing people to prioritise online leads, so that the valuable acquisition time and investment is not lost.

Attribution modelling

In this book we have looked at the various digital assets with which you can attract leads to your business: social media, websites, online advertising, email marketing, and so on, which at this stage prompts a key question:

What digital asset generates the most sales?

Attribution modelling is used widely in marketing to help businesses understand which tactics, channels and media work best to drive revenue. If email is more successful, you will want to put more resources into email. If online advertising delivers the most sales, then you will want to focus more on online advertising. However, a potential problem with attribution arises where you are using multiple digital channels to drive sales. How, at quarter end, do you determine the return from each channel and work out if and how you need to adjust your strategy?

Attributing revenue to each channel is important when it comes resource allocation, such as time commitment, staff reward and channel management. You want to avoid putting resources into digital assets that don't make money for you. You want to focus on those that do yield good revenue.

To do this, you must, choose your measurement of success. You might define success as the number of potential customers you have reached, or the number of unique visits to a page of your website, or the number of repeat sales you got, or the number of requests for information received through a digital channel.

As we have seen, you can work out the effectiveness of a digital media channel by using the tracking software available on, social media platforms, Google Analytics on your own website and also, by using tracking software such as Tweetdeck, Kongalytics, and Klout.

Help people to buy

A company should aim to keep communication between themselves and the customer simple so that the customer can easily access the information that they require within that crucial five-minute window. Live chat and chatbots are ideal for interfacing with the customer immediately. Live chat is widely available and chatbots are new technology that will rapidly come on-stream. Even setting up an automated response email for customer queries can help establish a connection with customers.

Throughout their marketing communications, 123.ie presents purchase options in a way that makes them easy to respond to. Emails and other correspondence is personalised. For example: 'Patrick, choose from our four cover options.'

Customers are presented with specific purchase options. There is no ambiguity about how you can proceed with buying insurance or contacting the company for more detailed information. Everything is laid out clearly for the customer.

Relentless focus on the needs of the customer will bring you from a position of selling to customers to a position of helping customers buy. Make that user experience as easy and enjoyable as possible.

Your content management and e-commerce system are critical for sales. Keep up with trends and developments; customers want the best experience available and they expect you to use the latest technology in your online offering and store.

**GOOD ONLINE
EXPERIENCE**

FAST PAGE LOADING
TIMES

PRODUCT COMPARISON

SIMPLE CHOICE

EASY SITE NAVIGATION

LIVE CHAT

SINGLE-ACTION ORDERING

AVAILABILITY OF STOCK

PRODUCT
RECOMMENDATIONS

PRODUCTS/SERVICES PURCHASED
BY SIMILAR CUSTOMERS

EMBEDDED VIDEO TO
ILLUSTRATE THE PRODUCT
IN MORE DETAIL

PAYMENT SECURITY
REASSURANCE

HOW TO CONTACT CUSTOMERS

Preferred communication:

- Business to consumer –
  both phone and email responses
  to queries work equally well.

- Business to business –
  business people prefer phone
  call responses.

Best time to contact:

- Wednesdays and Thursdays
  are the best days to call
  (49.7% better than the worst day).

- 4pm to 6pm are the best
  times to contact a lead
  (114% over the worst time,
  right after lunch).

- 8–9am and 4–5pm are the best
  times to call to qualify a lead,
  or set an appointment with a lead
  (164% better than 1–2pm,
  the worst time).

Upsell

One-off sales are like bread and jam, instantly satisfying, but not long-term staples. You have to be aware of the long-term value of customers and work hard to win their loyalty over time. So don't aim for a single sale; aim to build relationships online in exactly the same way as you would in a professional service or a high-end store.

Try to obtain your new customer's permission to keep them in touch with future offers. Permission email marketing, covered in **Chapter 6**, discusses various methods of emailing and keeping in touch without being disruptive or intrusive and can be used in upselling.

Another effective tactic for maximising the value of leads is to make further suggestions for purchase, based on the activity of other customers. For example, you might direct customers to purchases made by other customers who made a similar purchase. A customer-friendly tactic, and a way to get them back on your site, is to offer money off future purchases.

Remarket

Though we looked at remarketing in **Chapter 5**, it is worth mentioning here again because it is not only a way to advertise, it is also a way to capture and convert valuable leads.

You can use remarketing to remind prospective customers of their visit to your site. Remarketing keeps your website top of mind for customers and is often seen as more appropriate than general advertising because it closely matches the requirements of the individual. Here is an overview of remarketing by Google:

"Remarketing lets you show ads to people who have visited your website or used your mobile app before. When people leave your website without buying anything, for example, remarketing helps you reconnect with them by showing relevant ads as they browse the web, as they use mobile apps, or as they search on Google. Dynamic remarketing takes remarketing to the next level by including the products or services that people viewed on your website within the ads. While dynamic remarketing takes additional steps such as adding custom parameters to your website's tag and creating a feed, it can deliver customized, higher-performance ads."

GOOGLE.COM, 'USE REMARKETING TO REACH PAST WEBSITE VISITORS AND APP USERS'.

AT A GLANCE   CHAPTER NINE

We have arrived at the lead conversion chapter. This is your opportunity to convert leads into sales and revenue. Do you have the systems in place to capture leads, when they arrive into your inbox, on to your website or follow you on Twitter? Most businesses focus more on driving leads than they do on converting them. So, many warm leads are lost in cyberspace.

The best way to treat leads is to respond to them quickly, ideally within five minutes. The insurance company 123.ie are strong on driving and converting leads and they make doing business with them as easy as possible. Look at your business strategically. How can you make it easy to do business for your customers?

Once you have your customers, are there ways to strengthen the relationship? Upselling is important now – to provide incentives for future purchases and to develop loyalty.

The cost to acquire a customer is a sales cost and your online investments should be sales driven. Work out which of your digital assets attract the most sales and measure their performance from a revenue perspective. Remember to also focus on the long-term value of a customer. One-off sales are like bread and jam – instantly satisfying, but not long-term staples.

CHAPTER TEN
E-COMMERCE

10

Irish consumers spend €850,000 an hour online, which makes the Irish digital economy one of the fastest growing economies in the world, according to an Indecon report in May 2016. Irish SMEs are way beyond their European counterparts when it comes to e-commerce. The Irish digital economy employs over 116,000 people.

What is e-commerce?

Electronic commerce or e-commerce is the process of trading over the Internet. Here are some facts about e-commerce in Ireland.

According to the European Commission's *Europe's Digital Progress Report 2017* (EDPR – Ireland Profile), the Trading Online Voucher Scheme continues to be a popular initiative for Irish business. Over 2,600 businesses have participated so far. The scheme offers financial assistance, training and advice to small businesses to help them develop e-commerce capabilities (see localenterprise.ie). Participating businesses reported sales increases on average by 21%, with an 84% jump in sales leads. 60% began to export for the first time.

E-commerce accounts for 19% of Irish SMEs overall trade, compared to 9.4% for the EU, according to 2016 EDPR. However, as I mentioned throughout the book, businesses with fewer than 10 employees tend to be more reticent about setting up online sales capability.

While Irish consumers are spending online, Irish businesses are selling online but not in the same proportion. How do you capture some of that €7.5 billion consumer spending power?

Now we turn to the final, but still important, element of the online sales process – your systems, operations and processes – your e-commerce business. We begin with two e-commerce case studies – one American and one Irish.

FIGURE 10.1 — IRISH CONSUMERS: ONLINE SALES FACTS
(SOURCES: INDECON ECONOMIC CONSULTANTS REPORT 2016; DOT.IE DIGITAL HEALTH INDEX Q4 2017; CONSUMER MARKET MONITOR 2017 (MARKETING INSTITUTE OF IRELAND AND UCD)

IRISH CONSUMERS: ONLINE SALES FACTS

The value of Ireland's Internet economy is expected to reach €21.4 billion by 2020.

78% of Irish people make payments and bank online by mobile.

84% of Irish consumers bank online.

54% of Irish consumers click and collect.

94% of Irish consumers shop online.

90% of customers research a business online.

60% of Irish online spend goes abroad.

CASE STUDY ZAPPOS.COM — In 1999, a highly successful entrepreneur named Tony Hsieh bought into Zappos, an online shoe company in financial difficulty. Seeking funding to develop and expand was difficult and the main stumbling block was what Zappos sold. Investors resisted. Who buys shoes online? Don't people have to try on shoes for size? Aren't the costs of shipping and warehousing shoes prohibitive?

However, Tony Hsieh believed in Zappos. Within 10 years, the company's value rose from zero to a billion dollars. It seems people were happy to buy shoes online after all.

Tony's prior experience as an entrepreneur had taught him a valuable lesson: business success is all about happy people. Customers have to be happy. Employees have to be happy. Suppliers have to be happy. Those in charge of the organisation have to be happy. The only way to deliver a successful business online is to be entirely people-focused. The Zappos company motto, 'Happiness in a Box', means that processes, procedures and operations have to be tailored to the needs and the happiness of the customer.

In setting out to create a positive customer experience, sometimes you can just get lucky. Although in my experience, luck never really comes without hard work and innovative thinking. This is particularly true in this story about Funky Christmas Jumpers, an Irish company set up by Fabio Molle.

CASE STUDY FUNKY CHRISTMAS JUMPERS — Fabio and his team had been in touch with the entourage teams of a number of prominent Irish celebrities. One of those was Niall Horan of One Direction. When Niall needed a solution to a Christmas time wardrobe quandary, his personal assistant contacted Fabio Molle at Funky Christmas Jumpers. Fabio brought a selection of jumpers to where Niall Horan was staying and he was invited to stay for lunch.

An hour later, out went Niall Horan in his home-town of Mullingar in a trendy reindeer Christmas jumper – with lights and all. He was photographed sporting this wonderful Funky Christmas jumper. Images of the jumper appeared on Twitter and Facebook all over the world.

The following morning, the reindeer jumper sold out almost instantly as One Direction fans rushed to the online store to purchase the festive knitwear preferred by their idol.

FIGURE 10.2 — THREE LESSONS FROM THE SUCCESS OF ZAPPOS.COM
AND FUNKY CHRISTMAS JUMPERS

ZAPPOS.COM, FUNKY CHRISTMAS JUMPERS		
CUSTOMER HAPPINESS	OPERATIONS	THINKING BIG

Customer happiness

Customer happiness is not usually associated with operations and order processing, yet the best companies use customer happiness to drive every element of their value chain – from warehousing and distribution to invoicing and follow-up service. (Tony Hsieh even wrote a book on how to service customers entitled *Delivering Happiness*.)

Operations

As Zappos developed its 24-hour call-centre operation, it removed the restrictive policies common in similar customer service operations. Zappos employees are not asked to stick to scripts, are encouraged to make decisions without consulting managers and even

to send personal notes and flowers to customers. They are given optimised control of their role and the ability to deliver an excellent service for customers.

Thinking big

Zappos grew from zero to $10 billion and Funky Christmas Jumpers is a small business selling globally online. Don't be afraid to think big.

Manage your processes and your finances with the best advice available but think big and go for the widest market you can. The Internet facilitates that.

One of the greatest challenges, and opportunities for SMEs in Ireland is to grasp and embrace the concept of the online store. **Figure 10.3** below features six key elements of selling online.

FIGURE 10.3 — SIX KEY ELEMENTS OF SELLING ONLINE

Your online store

There are many online store options and systems choices. You may choose to take sales orders, have a booking or reservations system or to acquire the full retail store capability. In making your decision, it is worth considering the following:

- Specify the reports and information that you need to help build your business.
- Make sure that your online retail system can provide insights to help you with stocking, marketing and payments handling.
- Research your competitors and what they provide.
- Examine your customer profile and work out what technology and features they expect.
- Look at research about what is coming down the line.
- Make sure that you adopt a system that can easily adapt to future trends.

Set out in the following are key options available when setting up an online store.

Booking and reservation systems

As mentioned in **Chapter 7**, salon and hotel owners, restaurateurs and other service providers use 'off-the-shelf' online booking services. Consider the off-the-shelf options available for your business. For example, as a local product provider you may find that a 'click and collect' service is the best option for your customers.

Buy now buttons

'Buy Now' buttons can be added easily to websites and are a simple and cost-effective way for businesses to take payments without having to set up a full online store.

If you want to add a 'Buy Now' button to your existing website, then e-commerce platform providers such as Shopify, PayPal, Product Cart, CubeCart and AdobeMuse work well. PayPal even provide a copy and paste code for your 'Buy Now' button.

Hosted SaaS shopping carts

A full e-commerce solution for your business that can create an online store hosted in the cloud, can be provided by software as a service (SaaS) companies. Using their templates you can develop your website from scratch and include an online store.

Such development and hosting options have led to a significant decrease in the cost of developing an online store. They are often based on off-the-shelf templates available from the basic offering – with add-ons and customised solutions available at a higher cost under the premium modules. Most hosted solutions offer add-ons such as payments gateways (see **page 96**), shipping services and stock management systems.

Note that online shopping store software providers do not provide the systems and facilities for processing payments. Your online payments provider is a separate entity that handles the security and processing of the entire financial transaction, including foreign currency exchange. Online payments options are outlined under 'Payments handling' on **page 96**.

Self-hosted software

Another, more advanced option is to install the software on your own website and host your own online store. For this you will need to work with developers to design and amend the online shopping experience you offer your customers. As mentioned above, you will also need to add and provide payment facilities for your online store.

With the self-hosting option, you are in control of your own branding and can make enhancements as you go, which is a positive aspect. However, if you experience problems with your online store, it is more difficult to resolve them than if your store is hosted by an expert website-hosting company.

You are also responsible for security, fraud prevention and resolution of all issues that arise. This can be complicated for a small business and in the case of fraud and security issues could also be costly.

Most small businesses would be advised to use an externally hosted service.

Online marketplaces

You can also sell through ready-made marketplaces such as those offered by Amazon, Etsy, Ebay and so on. While you benefit from economies of scale and an established set of customers, there are also down sides. Online marketplaces can be costly, crowded and it may be difficult to establish your brand above the marketplace owner, such as Amazon.

On the positive side, you have a shop window, payment processing and fraud protection already set up for you. Set up cost is low though there are fees, charges and commissions.

Mobile e-commerce

Mobile e-commerce, takes place using mobile devices. Social media sites such as Facebook and Instagram are important drivers of e-commerce.

Think 'mobile first'. Make sure that whatever online sales, booking or reservation systems you choose work well on smart phones.

Payments handling

When dealing with payments systems, there are critical decisions that you have to make – for example, whether payments will be processed on your server or remotely. There are security implications if payments are processed on your site, and this solution is more suitable to large-volume transactions and larger organisations.

Merchant account and payment gateway

A merchant account is a bank account that allows you to accept credit card payments. This you can get from your business banking team.

The payment gateway is a payments processing service that links your merchant bank account to your online store. The payment gateway is similar to the point of sale (POS) machine that retailers have instore that processes the customer card and sends the funds to the retailer's bank account. There are fees associated with both merchant accounts and with payment gateways. It is worth shopping around for a gateway because fees and charges vary and will depend on your particular requirements.

Shipping

There is no point getting online orders unless you can ship and deliver efficiently, effectively and quickly.

As part of your online store, you can integrate a shipping functionality in association with a carrier such as An Post, DHL or UPS. A good distribution company will provide a full online service and enable you to print labels, schedule parcel pick-up and track the parcel internationally.

It is important to be aware of e-commerce law, such as customer rights to return goods (see **page 98**), as well as tax laws relating to VAT when shipping abroad.

"When connecting with customers, it is the small things that matter. Empowering the people who run your warehouse to compose and include kind notes with products is a small thing – but it matters. Empowering your distribution staff to upgrade customers to faster shipping for free makes a hugely positive impact on customers and that matters."

LILLIAN VERNON

Communication

Customer service, shipping and delivery are closely related. Keep a sharp eye on your customers' orders. When you become aware of a delay, inform the customer immediately. Funky Christmas Jumpers track orders very carefully and, although it can be extremely busy at peak pre-Christmas time, they keep in touch with customers to make sure that they meet shipping expectations. At peak times, Fabio Molle stays up all night to answer questions from Australian and American customers. This determination to maintain a high level of customer service results in a high level of trust. High trust results in repeat orders. Customer service is critical to online sales.

Returns

In order to boost customer confidence and for online retailing to really work, it must be possible for customers to return items if they are not exactly what they wanted. Most online retailers offer a no-quibble returns policy. However, returns are also one of the greatest negatives for selling goods online.

Consumer rights and protection are an important part of handling returned goods and in dealing with customer complaints. When you set up an online store, make sure that you are familiar with the rights of both you and the consumer.

IF AN OUTLET OFFERS FREE RETURNS, THE AVERAGE RATE OF RETURNS WILL BE

31-33%

IF THE CUSTOMER HAS TO INCUR THE POSTAGE COST, RETURN RATES DROP TO

21-24%

CLOTHING CAN HAVE A RETURNS RATE AS HIGH AS 70%. THE AVERAGE RATE IS

45-50%

ELECTRONICS HAVE ONE OF THE LOWEST RETURNS RATES WITH AN AVERAGE OF

7-9%

(SOURCE: DIGITAL MARKETING INSTITUTE REPORT IN ASSOCIATION WITH AHAIN GROUP: SOCIAL BUSINESS: ECOMMERCE AND THE DIGITAL DYNASTY 2013)

CONSUMER RIGHTS AND PROTECTION

Set out below are outlines of key pieces of legislation with which your business must comply if it is selling goods or services to consumers, and furthermore if it is doing so online ('distance selling'). It is recommended that you get legal advice to ensure that your business fully complies with the law.

1. THE CONSUMER PROTECTION ACT 2007 AND THE COMPETITION AND CONSUMER PROTECTION ACT 2014.

Relating to unfair commercial practices, consumer protection and competition laws, the Competition and Consumer Protection Commission oversees the implementation of these laws. The aim of the Commission is to make markets work better for consumers and businesses. It ensures that all marketing is fair and honest in its representation of products and services, including:
- product characteristics and features;
- origin of products;
- availability of goods;
- quantity, risks;
- ingredients; and
- after-sales service.

More information is available at: www.citizensinformation.ie

2. EUROPEAN DIRECTIVE ON CONSUMER RIGHTS (DIRECTIVE 2011/83/EU) (KNOWN AS THE CONSUMER RIGHTS DIRECTIVE).

'Distance selling' involves communication between a business and a consumer where they are not in each other's physical presence and includes purchases made by e-mail, telephone, Internet shopping and mail order.

When a customer enters into a distance contract with an online seller, they have the right to expect the same consumer protection as they would if they bought the goods in a local shop. The goods should be of merchantable quality, fit for the purpose intended and as described. Because the consumer is entering into a distance contract, they have additional protection under EU law.

The Consumer Rights Directive aims to ensure that consumers can expect the same minimum level of protection no matter where a trader is based in the EU.

More information is available at: www.citizensinformation.ie

3. EUROPEAN UNION (CONSUMER INFORMATION, CANCELLATION AND OTHER RIGHTS) REGULATIONS 2013 (SI NO. 484 OF 2013).

These regulations give effect in Ireland to Directive 2011/83/EU on Consumer Rights. The regulations came into operation on 13 June 2014 and apply to contracts concluded after that date.

Subject to specified exclusions, the regulations:
- set out the substance and form of the information that traders must provide to consumers before consumers are bound by on-premises, off-premises or distance contracts;
- give consumers the right to cancel off-premises and distance contracts within 14 days of the delivery of the goods in the case of sales contracts and 14 days of the conclusion of the contract in the case of service contracts;
- regulate the fees charged by traders in respect of the use of a given means of payment, the cost of calls by consumers to customer helplines, and payments by consumers additional to the remuneration agreed for the trader's main obligation under the contract;
- amend the provisions of the Sale of Goods Act 1893 on the passing of risk, and certain of the Act's rules on delivery, in contracts of sale where the buyer deals as consumer.

More information is available at: www.dbei.gov.ie

4. SALE OF GOODS AND SUPPLY OF SERVICES ACT 1980.

Consumer contracts are protected under Irish and EU law. Online sellers in Ireland must comply with the Sale of Goods and Supply of Services Act 1980.

Under this Act, the purchaser of goods or services has a number of rights, including that goods must be of merchantable quality, services should be fully carried out, goods and services should be fit for purpose and provided as described by a salesperson or an advertisement.

More information is available at: www.citizensinformation.ie

After-sales service

Zappos put a lot of marketing effort into the after-sale experience of their customers. They operate a 24/7 warehouse and, in the US, orders placed before midnight are often received by the purchaser the next morning.

Research tells the Zappos team that each customer contacts the Zappos call centre, on average, once in their lifetime. Zappos maximises the opportunity to create a positive lasting impression from that one call. They see every piece of correspondence as an opportunity to build a relationship.

Small, meaningful offerings of goodwill can make a noticeable difference to a relationship – whether they involve shipping upgrades, product samples, an extra discount or an extra piece of cheese on a sandwich. This is the personal touch that creates the personality of your business.

AT A GLANCE   CHAPTER TEN

Research makes it clear that Irish consumers are spending money online and that Irish businesses are competing well in the digital space when compared to their European counterparts. At the same time, according to IEDR, 60% of Irish SMEs cannot take orders online and consumers are buying from businesses abroad as a result.

Many businesses are daunted by the level of investment of money, resources and time it takes to set up an online store. There is a range of options for setting up online selling and each option can integrate online payment facilities – making the prospect of opening an online store more possible and less difficult.

Reliable, fast delivery is important to consumers. There are great distribution companies that have developed to support the rise of online selling. Most provide valuable related services including label printing, scheduling and tracking of packages.

Returns will always be a costly part of online selling and consumers expect to be able to return goods without penalty.

When you do decide to enter the e-commerce realm, or if you are already there, your systems, operations and processing procedures are critical.

In this phase of your business, your mind should always be on the big prize: developing a healthy and loyal customer base who advocates for your business.

The aim of this book is to help you navigate the online space from understanding the customer to developing your digital assets right through to your e-commerce proposition.

I wish you great success in your digital marketing journey.

APPENDIX A
DATA PROTECTION (GDPR)

Introduction

In force from 25 May 2018, the General Data Protection Regulation (GDPR) and its requirements are particularly important in the context of digital marketing. As a business operating in the world of digital marketing and sales, it is critical that you get legal advice on your obligations to comply with the GDPR and that you have the right processes in place to demonstrate that you are compliant. While I have summarised some of the key considerations below, each business should get advice that is tailored to their specific circumstances, activities and requirements.

THE GENERAL DATA PROTECTION REGULATION (GDPR) The GDPR replaces previous data protection legislation across the EU, which was out of date, written as it was before mass Internet and mobile connectivity. Data protection concerns the protection of 'personal data', which means "any information relating to an identified or identifiable natural person" (the 'data subject').

Organisations, including businesses, that gather, store and/or otherwise 'process' personal data have a legal obligation to safeguard the privacy of the individuals with whose data they are entrusted. The right to privacy is a fundamental human right and if affects all of us. The GDPR is intended to further ensure that this right to privacy is protected by placing stricter measures on businesses to protect personal data. It requires businesses to carefully consider their need for personal data, that the gathering and processing of that personal data be appropriate to that need, and that personal data only be used for the stated intended purpose when it was originally given by the individual (consumer).

DIRECT MARKETING AND CONSENT Direct marketing is one of the areas most impacted by the GDPR. Together with the Privacy and Electronic Communications Regulations (PECR) the GDPR gives consumers specific privacy rights in relation to electronic communications.

One of the fundamental principles of the GDPR is that organisations must have a legal basis for processing personal data and the legal basis likely to be most relevant to a business involved in direct marketing, digitally or otherwise, is **consent**.

The GDPR defines "the consent of the data subject" as "any freely given specific and informed indication of his wishes by which the data subject signifies his agreement to personal data relating to him being processed".

That means that when you engage in digital marketing – be it emails, SMS messages, newsletters, for example, then you need to carefully consider the legal basis for obtaining, using and retaining the personal data with which you market to individuals. You must inform the data subject that you intend to market to them when you collect their details, you must have the data subjects' valid consent to receive this marketing material, and this consent must be unambiguous and by way of "a statement or by a clear affirmative action". Pre-ticked boxes and 'implied consent' are no longer acceptable.

You must also make it easy for data subjects to exercise their right to withdraw their consent at any time. Consent should be separate from other terms and conditions and should not generally be a pre-condition of signing up to a service. You must keep clear records to demonstrate consent.

Further digital marketing considerations

Clearly, the above applies to direct marketing: before you include a person on your email marketing database, you must make sure that their personal email addresses, contact details and information is lawfully collected and stored and that unambiguous consent is received and retrievable.

In this book, I have discussed extensively the personalised nature of digital marketing. Personalisation is an important feature of digital marketing and it tends to appeal to consumers – once it is used respectfully. However, the various digital marketing tools that enable you to personalise campaigns are now answerable to the requirements of the GDPR and must be managed carefully to ensure that users' privacy and data protection rights are observed. Here are some elements to consider:

- The privacy policy of your business should outline what data you are collecting, why (for what purpose) and how long it will be held for. Be up front: your privacy policy should be on your website and it must be in an obvious place, not hidden in the 'Terms & Conditions'.
- **Google Analytics** and **Google AdWords** use cookies to track user information that informs marketing strategies, conversions and campaigns. Google's data can also be used to create 'remarketing' ads that follow consumer activity as they move around the web. Cookies can also be used in social media advertising.

Users can change their settings to stop this tracking by turning on 'Do not track'. Once that functionality is turned on then the user is not identifiable.

As a marketer, you must make users aware of your use of cookies on your website, which means that you should:

- state your use of cookies in your privacy policy;
- explain why cookies and other tracking tools are used, including for remarketing ads, if relevant or applicable;
- allow users to explicitly agree to use of cookies and tracking;
- require users to opt in; and
- allow users to opt out at any time.

It is worth looking at PayPal's cookie policy page for an example of how this is done well.

Existing customers

It is understood that under the GDPR, a 'soft opt-in' option is applicable for existing customers, meaning a business can send existing customers emails, text, etc., if:

- it obtained their contact details in the course of a sale to that person in the previous 12 months;
- the business is promoting its own, similar products or services;
- the data subject was offered a simple opportunity to opt-out, both when first collecting their details and in subsequent marketing.

How to comply with the GDPR

The GDPR requires businesses to review and update their processes in handling personal data and to be able to demonstrate their compliance with the legislation. The following sets out measures that should be taken to ensure that you comply with the GDPR in your digital marketing:

REVIEW ALL PERSONAL DATA HELD BY YOUR BUSINESS Review all the personal data that you hold on behalf of customers (existing and prospective). Map out precisely how you acquired this data, your purposes for collecting it, how you use and process it, how your store it and for how long. How you make it secure and with whom you share it is important too.

ENSURE THE PERSONAL DATA YOU HOLD IS HELD LAWFULLY Review the data that you hold for each of your customers. Make sure that data held for each individual is lawful and that you have their consent to hold that information. You may have to get retrospective consent from some of your customers.

'PRIVACY BY DESIGN' The GDPR introduces the concept of 'privacy by design', meaning that you should embed consideration of customers' right to privacy and safeguarding of their personal data into your systems and processes, emphasising the importance of consent, allowing customers to opt in and opt out of receiving communications from your business.

'PRIVACY BY DEFAULT' Privacy by default requires organisations to ensure that through their technical processes and systems, only personal data that is necessary for a specific purpose is processed.

DATA PROTECTION AND DATA RETENTION POLICIES Create appropriate data protection and data retention policies for your business. Review and update your employment contracts and employee handbook to include these data policies.

ENSURE THAT PERSONAL DATA IS STORED SECURELY AND PROTECTED AGAINST DATA BREACH Measures you can take regarding data security include: strong password policies; encrypting PCs, laptops, smartphones, memory sticks, etc.; regular back-up of data to a server located off-site or 'in the cloud'; checking the physical security of your offices; and staff training about data protection and security.

REVIEW ALL COMPANY CONTRACTS TO ENSURE THAT THEY ARE GDPR-COMPLIANT Review all contracts with suppliers, and partner organisations, with whom you may share personal data and make sure you have third-party data-processor agreements in place.

ENSURE YOU HAVE PROCEDURES IN PLACE TO MANAGE AND RESPOND TO DATA SUBJECT REQUESTS You must facilitate the right of each individual to access personal data relating to them, that is held by you, to amend that data or to have it erased (the 'right to be forgotten').

BE PREPARED FOR A DATA BREACH It is vital to understand and think through what constitutes a data breach. All businesses must put in place a process for flagging, escalating and dealing with a data breach. The GDPR stipulates strict response times to a data breach. Among your team, training is important. Generate a culture of awareness and responsibility, so that employees are very aware of what a data breach is and that they are comfortable disclosing and responding to a data error.

UPDATE YOUR PRIVACY POLICY Privacy policy notices online should be detailed and easily accessible for customers and prospects. Your privacy policy must clearly identify your business, how data is obtained, and how it will be used and retained. I mentioned above that your privacy policy should highlight cookies used to track online behaviour and how those cookies are used. It must also provide details of a complaints procedure.

The consequences of non-compliance

The GDPR gives enhanced powers to the Data Protection Commissioner (DPC) and enhances the rights of data subjects. The DPC now has the power to impose fines on any company found to be in breach of the GDPR, including administrative failures, such as failing to maintain adequate records demonstrating consent. Fines can be up to €20 million or 4% of turnover, whichever is greater.

Perhaps of more concern for most SMEs, given their size, is that data subjects have a new right to sue the company for infringement of their rights under the GDPR and seek compensation in the courts. Effectively a new area of litigation, cases could involve a number of data subjects taking a legal action at the same time for the same breach or loss.

GDPR and SMEs

While SMEs may be exempt from some of the more rigorous requirements of the GDPR, including the appointment of a data protection officer, if an SME is contracting, for example as a data processor, with a larger company that must comply with the GDPR in full, then the SME may also have to be fully compliant.

Larger companies dealing with an SME may require the smaller business to be fully compliant. Conversely, if an SME can demonstrate to a large business client that they are fully compliant, the SME will have a competitive advantage.

REFERENCES

Amárach Consulting, *Connected Futures – Bridging Ireland's Urban-Rural Divide*, Vodafone Series, 2015.

Amárach Consulting, *The Three Connected Ireland Report*, October 2017.

Berger, J. and Milkman, K., *"What makes Online Content Viral?"*, Journal of Marketing Research, April 2012.

Brandt, Richard L., *One Click – Jeff Bezos and the Rise of Amazon.com* (Portfolio Penguin, 2011).

Court, D., Gordon, J., and Perrey, J., *"Measuring Marketing's Worth"*, McKinsey Quarterly, May 2012.

Day, G., *"Is it Real? Can we win? Is it worth doing? Managing Risk and Reward in an Innovation Portfolio"*, Harvard Business Review, December 2007.

Deloitte Ireland, *Global Mobile Consumer Survey – The Irish Cut* (2017).

Digital Marketing Institute Report in association with Ahain Group: *Social Business: eCommerce and the Digital Dynasty* (2013).

eir Connected Living Survey, 2015. Conducted by Behaviour and Attitudes.

Eptica, *Multichannel Experience Study* 2016.

Krogue, K., *"Why Companies Waste 71% of Internet Leads"*, Forbes, July 2012.

Hsieh, T., *Delivering Happiness: A Path to Profits, Passion and Purpose* (Business Plus 2010).

IAB Ireland, *PwC Online Adspend Study*, April 2016.

IEDR, *dot ie Digital Health Index*, Q4 2017, conducted by Ignite Research. See www.iedr.ie/why-choose-ie/digital-health-index.

Indecon International Economic Consultants, *Assessment of the Macro-Economic Impact of Internet/Digital on the Irish Economy*, prepared for the Department of Communications, Energy & Natural Resources, March 2016. See www.indecon.ie.

Forrester, *Introducing the Forrester Wave: Digital Asset Management* (Q3 2016).

Ipsos MORI Social Networking Tracker 2017.

Irish Life – iReach Survey 2017.

Jones, M., *"Emotional Engagement is Key to Viral Content Marketing"*, Social Media Today, November 2012.

Kim, W. Chan and Mauborgne, R., *Blue Ocean Strategy: How to Create Uncontested Market Space and Make the Competition Irrelevant* (Harvard Business School Publishing, 2015).

Mediacom Ireland, *Social Nation* (November 2017).

Reuters Institute for the Study of Journalism, *Reuters Institute Digital News Report 2016*.

Safko, L., *The Social Media Bible – Tactics, Tools and Strategies for Business Success*, (John Wiley & Sons, 2012).

Scott, David M., *The New Rules of Marketing and PR: How to Use Social Media, Online Video, Mobile Applications, Blogs, News Releases and Viral Marketing to Reach Buyers Directly* (John Wiley & Sons, 2015).

Smith, A., "A 'Week in the Life': Analysis of Smartphone Users", Chapter 3 in *U.S. Smartphone Use in 2015* (Pew Research Center, April 2015). See www.pewinternet.org.

Department of Communications, Energy & Natural Resources, *Growing Small Business through Online Trade: Enterprise Impacts of the Trading Online Voucher Scheme* (May 2016).

Vogel, D. R., Dickson, G. W. and Lehman, J. A., *Persuasion and the Role of Visual Presentation Support: The UM/M Study* (Management Information Systems Research Center, University of Minnesota, June 1986).